Ohio Traffic Tickets are for the Birds

Ohio Traffic Tickets are for the Birds

A Practical Defense Manual for Juveniles and Adults

Brian Jonathan Wolk

Writers Club Press
New York   Lincoln   Shanghai

Ohio Traffic Tickets are for the Birds
A Practical Defense Manual for Juveniles and Adults

Writers Club Press
an imprint of iUniverse, Inc.

For information address:
iUniverse
2021 Pine Lake Road, Suite 100
Lincoln, NE 68512
www.iuniverse.com

ISBN: 0-595-21521-1

Printed in the United States of America

Dedication

For my wife Jodi, the eternal love of my life…in this world and the next.

For my Father and Mother, who taught me the two keys to happiness are independence and patience.

For my brother Ron, the idea man, who taught me that a car is much more than just something to get you from point A to point B.

For my sister Cindy, who taught me how to drive…including how to do 360s!

Epigraph

Regardless of nationality, everyone who drives in Africa drives like this—with heat-inspired, desperate, pedal-to-the-floor insanity, heedless of reason, of their own or anyone else's desire to live beyond the next turn. The driver becomes the vehicle, soaking up the power—enjoying it mentally and physically—lusting for the freedom of unregulated roads. Speed limits are not enforced. He drives as if life must be chased mercilessly to its end and finished in a bright flash…a rogue folk hero: adventurous, kind, cruel, and selfless all at once. A bit like the contradictions inherent in the American cowboy myth—the free-spirited, big-hearted soul with a malicious edge. The drivers, too, are struggling to survive.

—Peter Chilson, *Riding the Demon*

Contents

Preface

Most citizens get their first real spectacle of the legal system in traffic court. After seeing it operate on them or their loved ones, their rose-colored glasses view of government more often than not begins fading to black.

Why did I write this book? You would think it's because there isn't a book out there specifically addressing Ohio traffic tickets, or that there isn't even a book out there effectively addressing the proper method for fighting traffic tickets *in general*, no matter what state, and finally that there isn't a book out there addressing juvenile traffic offenders—though juvenile traffic court rules, procedures, fines, trials and sentences are separate and distinct from their adult counterparts.

That's *part* of the reason I wrote this book. But there's something more important that needs consideration. And it's this: **we need a reformation in our way of thinking about government.**

To clarify my point, a few incidents deserve consideration. *Inter alia,* they reveal a pattern of arbitrary local governmental enforcement of traffic regulations.

Call the first incident 'Ticket-gate' to help explain. As of midsummer 2001, in Plain Township alone—a small part of Stark County, Ohio—there were at least forty (40) roads with *illegally posted* traffic signs. And they had been *illegally posted for forty (40) years.* Forty signs, forty years. And that's only in Plain Township. Imagine how many signs like this there are throughout Ohio and other states! People were being given

xii Ohio Traffic Tickets are for the Birds

citations based on these traffic signs, but these people weren't breaking any law, because the traffic signs were illegal. What's more, when told these speed restrictions were invalid, local government kept the traffic signs up and *continued imposing them* on people.[1] They suspended the laws, using the guise of *public safety* as their sword and shield, in direct contravention of Section 18 of Article I (Bill of Rights) of the Constitution of the State of Ohio, which provides, "No power of suspending laws shall ever be exercised, except by the general assembly."

What does this government abuse amount to in solely monetary terms? Consider a low-estimate example: 40 roads, 40 years, one ticket per road per week at $25 per ticket, equals *2.08 million.* Try your own calculation. If we use the more reasonable 5 tickets per week at a cost of $50, then we get *$20.08 million,* unjustly taken from the people. This doesn't include increased insurance costs and license reinstitution fees.

Now you see why it's called Ticket-gate. Just wait until concerned, activist citizens press county engineers throughout the state of Ohio and other states to investigate *their* signs. Ticket-gate will prove a trifle in comparison.

The real tragedy? Those illegally posted signs, to my knowledge, hadn't been challenged once, *not once,* over those 40 years, and so the government got away with it.

Another eloquent example concerns the village (a mayor's court) of New Rome, Ohio on the outskirts of Columbus. Here a straightforward review reveals an even more appalling record of arbitrary governance regarding traffic ticket enforcement. In 2001, New Rome's revenue was $412,000. A full 92% of this came from traffic tickets.[2] All the while, the mayor's court clerk was stealing this traffic ticket money for her own use.[3]

New Rome's traffic ticket barrages contribute in small part to Ohio's accolade of being #1 in issuance of speeding tickets (Pennsylvania is #2).[4] The state of Ohio itself considers New Rome's speed limit illegal, but so far to no avail—according to Ohio Department of Transportation (ODOT) officials, ODOT doesn't have the authority to enforce a speed limit change, but their opinion could be taken in issue before a judge and used to bolster the argument.[5]

Numerous similar stories of improper executive enforcement of traffic laws crisscross the great state of Ohio, and this type of behavior is slowly becoming a national phenomenon.

A primary lesson may be grafted from this pattern—Unchecked power is self-corrupting. Its victims are your money and your rights. Its causes are unwarranted and incorrect assumptions: that government, if left alone, will necessarily act preventively and legally to protect us; that since the government is acting, it must be legal; that police officers don't make mistakes; that police officers and the government are to be feared; that we are guilty and have to prove ourselves innocent; that the laws are made to control we, the people, and not the government. Two words: *Fatally wrong.*

If you don't protect your own rights, nobody will. If you allow yourself to be arbitrarily governed in the 'small' things of life (truthfully though, traffic law indiscriminately affects us *all* in numerous, untold ways), then your temperament for self-rule and independence will surely fade. And that is an unacceptable disservice to yourself, your brothers and sisters, your mother, father, children, and your fellow citizens. If, on the other hand, you show attention to detail concerning your liberties, if you engage and encourage others to engage their spirit of self-government, then you serve yourself, your family and your country as well. You do an invaluable, though possibly unseen, service for the coming generations. Your reward isn't notoriety; your reward is liberty and the opportunity to pursue happiness.

Generally, the American ideal is that government must be made and kept accountable *in all things.* If it isn't, then it won't be. And in the field of traffic law, which is big business (and I emphasize *business*)—it isn't.

We are a government of the people by the people and for the people. Let's keep it that way. If only half the people ticketed simply pled not guilty or not true, the traffic court system would hemorrhage and shut down. And then, and only then, it would reform.

Alan Dershowitz espoused the *number one* controlling rule of the criminal process system as: "Most criminal defendants are, in fact, guilty."[6] Well, Mr. Dershowitz, as far as traffic criminal defendants are concerned, your rule is seriously mistaken. Perhaps that's the exception that he hadn't found for this, that exists for every rule…it is. As Mr. Dershowitz noted, benign corruption and cheating "is pervasive in our legal system—and everyone with any experience knows it."[7] The traffic regime affects *all* citizens, plays a heavy part in underground political campaigning, and produces substantial monetary intake for various governmental and non-governmental agencies. Traffic regimes are motivated as much by economic and political realities than legal or socially beneficial reasons. One can only wonder the amount of quality corruption.

The only viable countervailing reaction is citizen activism. *This* is the practical manual aiding the activist with regards to fighting traffic tickets. But, in the final analysis, it is the reader alone who must decide for her or himself whether to take the stand.

Section One

Introduction

1

The Method

You have a good chance of defeating your traffic ticket at or before trial, and at the very least of getting it reduced in sentence and/or fine. And you don't need a lawyer to do it. Here are the three reasons why.

PROOF: Make them prove it.

The prosecution (the government) bears the burden of proof. They have to prove you guilty *beyond a reasonable doubt*. This is the highest possible standard, so the slightest slip-up or *inconsistency* on their part can destroy their case, no matter how 'true' it is. Truth is *never* the issue in a court of law; don't let them fool you with their doubletalk that it is. The real issue is: can they prove you did all the elements of the charge beyond a reasonable doubt? That's the *real* legal and factual issue for the judge or jury to consider; they're charged to decide if the government has provided enough quality proof to prove that one of their fellow citizens has, beyond a reasonable doubt, committed every element of a crime. You (the Defense) don't have to do anything, and can focus on finding inconsistencies in their case. Remember, you're innocent until proven guilty. While the officer tickets you, you're innocent. While the prosecutor tries to rush you into a plea, saying they have a pretty good case, you're innocent. While you stand before the judge or magistrate at arraignment, you're innocent. While the prosecutor at trial is busy saying how guilty you are, you're innocent. You're innocent until proven guilty. Make them prove it.

PROCEDURES: Beat them with their own book of rules.

The government has placed a boatload of bureaucratic regulations on itself. In order to legally enforce your traffic ticket they must abide by these regulations. Here is another fact: government is inefficient. Doubtless you know this. It's one of the reasons people don't get involved with the machine in the first place, and just plead guilty...because they don't want to get stuck in the bureaucratic bayou. Combine these two facts (regulations and inefficiency), and what you get is one part of government passing numerous regulations while the other part is completely unaware of or doesn't have the resources to keep up with these regulations (or just doesn't care to!). This is a recipe for disaster, both for their case against you and protection of your civil liberties. The proper recourse is action. Make them prove they're abiding by these regulations. Beat them with their own book of rules.

PRACTICE: Let them use their experience against themselves.

Traffic ticket prosecutors are often green. They're often not even lawyers yet, but only legal interns doing a job that no one else wants or no 'respectable' lawyer would do. Sometimes, only the law enforcement officer is at court to present the government's case (then, you're almost *guaranteed* to win). At the same time, traffic trials represent some of the hardest cases to prosecute and win. Why? Because of the proof and procedures mentioned above. Combine these two facts (difficulty level and inexperience), and the chances mount that they'll make a fatal mistake at trial or before, leave out a necessary element of their case or not follow the regulations. The problem is that citizens without experience don't see these mistakes and oversights happening right before their very eyes, and so the government gets away with it. This book will open your eyes, you'll be able to see the mistakes and oversights, and be able to use them to win.

These are the three basics of any successful traffic ticket defense: Proof, Procedures, and Practice. The Method.

In applying them your core goal is *Producing Inconsistencies* in the government's case: the cracks of reasonable doubt in the prosecutor's house of evidence. Just one is enough to get your ticket thrown out (case dismissed).

Focus on these concepts, this method, and you stand a good chance of getting your case dismissed, or at the very least of getting a reduction in sentence and/or fine. You stand an even better chance of learning the law and protecting your and your fellow citizens' rights. It only remains to show you the details of the method, the how.

2

Before you begin

The symbol (§) means Section. Thus, "*See* §4511.21," means, "*See* Section 4511.21." I cite various particular rules or laws throughout the book in order to help those who want to get an official copy of the law. Here are some abbreviations I will use:

TR means, "Ohio Traffic Rules (of procedure)."

TL means, "Traffic Laws—Operation of Motor Vehicles."

ER means, "Ohio Rules of Evidence."

CR means, "Ohio Rules of Criminal Procedure."

JCR means, "Juvenile Court Rules."

JR means, "Ohio Rules of Juvenile Procedure."

This book covers misdemeanors, from the lowest classification of minor misdemeanors (MM) to the highest classification of misdemeanors of the first degree (M1). It's important that you find out the classification of your traffic violation, which depends on what violation it is and how many you've had before. The best ways of finding this out: (1) Call the prosecutor's office, find out who handles traffic ticket cases, and ask them what level it is, (2) Include this question in any requests you send the prosecutor.

Here's why it's important that you find out:

MM: No confinement, Maximum fine–$100

M4: Maximum confinement–30 days, Maximum fine–$250

M3: Maximum confinement–60 days, Maximum fine–$500

M2: Maximum confinement–90 days, Maximum fine–$750

M1: Maximum confinement–6 months, Maximum fine–$1,000

For juveniles, there are special fine allocations that modify the above system:

MM: Maximum fine–$50

M4: Maximum fine–$75

M3: Maximum fine–$125

M2: Maximum fine–$175

M1: Maximum fine–$250

In addition, for juveniles the court has other *discretionary* powers. For example, the court *may*, among other things, suspend your license, place you on probation, or make you pay for damages you caused. *See* §2151.356–JCR. Neither of the fine and sentence allocation systems listed above includes court costs, fines and additional penalties for failure to prove financial responsibility (*See* §4509.101 & §4509.99), or other *discretionary* fine or sentence allocation powers that the court may have, depending on the violation. For example, for street racing the court *may* suspend your driver license up to a year. *See* §4511.99(B)–TL. Or if you've failed to stop for a school bus, you may be fined up to $500. *See* §4511.99(G)–TL. There's also the issue of license points, which varies with the violation.

Finally, if you're an adult and your fine *could* exceed $100, then you have the right to a trial by jury. *See* §2945.17. To get a trial by jury you must demand it in writing. This writing must be filed with the clerk of courts not less than ten days prior to the date set for trial, or on or before the third day following receipt of notice of the date set for trial, whichever is later. If you don't demand it, you waive the right. *See* Rule 23–CR; Appendix on Forms, Jury Trial.

I think you get the point. It's important to find out the classification of your traffic violation. If nothing else, it will motivate you to be a smarter (which means better or *more clever*) driver.

3

Special advice to juveniles I

First off, and don't cringe, if you haven't already you need to tell your parents and/or guardians about your ticket. "Why?! So they can ground me, send me to my room and punish me on top of what the court might do!" Well…it's a thought, but no. Truth is, you might be surprised at how much your parents know, who they know, and how they can help you fight this ticket. You might also be surprised at what your parents *think* about this colossal traffic ticket scheme, and their own past 'run-ins with the law. It's good to get your parents/guardians involved, because though they're authority figures, they're authority figures *on your side*. And that's a good thing.

But if you *don't* tell them, and they find out later (which they usually do), not only will your punishment probably be worse than what you might have received initially, but you risk harming the basic trust that exists between you and your parents or guardians, and that's the most important thing. What's more, if the judge or magistrate finds out that you didn't tell your folks, then you risk their remedy being stricter than it would otherwise be.

If you're afraid they'll get mad, tell them, "Dad, Mom…I've got something I want to tell you, but first I want you to read this." Then let them read this chapter. I bet they'll smile, and I bet they'll be more understanding. That's because their *not* understanding and helping you is just as harmful to the trust-relationship as you not telling them. Right?

Afraid they won't let you fight the ticket? No way! Truth is (and you should definitely make your parents read this part), concertedly fighting a traffic ticket is one of the best ways for a young woman or man to learn about the judicial and legal system, to see how it works, how to analyze it, and to learn how to defend and protect those civil liberties that each of us has and often takes for granted. You'll learn a lot about yourself and your society. It's actually a good idea...but don't go out and get a ticket just so you can!

Section Two

Proof

4

To begin with

This section covers the general subject of proof: elements, evidence, and organization (matching). You must find out what the government has to prove beyond a reasonable doubt (**elements** of proof). Just as importantly, you must find out *how* they're going to do it. That is, you must get your hands on all the **evidence** the government has on your case. Thirdly, you must **organize** (match) these elements and evidence.

You can organize what the government has to prove by using the checklist format in the Appendix on Forms, and studying the chapter in this section covering what statutory section you were cited under. If you're so inclined, you can read the 'Procedures Section' first. Be sure to go *over* the Procedures Section before diving into your investigation. Both the Proof and Procedures sections will show you the most profitable areas for you to investigate, whether it is a witness' prior statements or the height of a speed limit sign.

This section cites a number of the more frequent laws (statutes) that police use in their citations, and goes over their general **elements**. If the statute you were cited under is not covered in this book, then you have a number of options: (1) Go to a law school in your area, tell the librarian (preferably the chief librarian, who is often a lawyer) you were cited for a traffic ticket, tell her what the section number is (for example,

§4513.24–TL), and ask where it can be found, (2) Use your local law library to try and find it. *See* Appendix, Helpful Contacts, (3) Request a copy of the section from the prosecutor. Whether or not this book considers the specific statute you were cited under, the general method still applies.

If you were cited under a local ordinance, this ordinance is required to be *substantially similar* to the analogous state traffic law. For example, §4511.21–TL concerns speed limits; so if you're cited under a local ordinance for speeding, you can use §4511.21 to organize your defense. Still, you should get a copy of the local ordinance from the police force that cited you (just call and ask), so that you can compare the two. They should be substantially similar; if not, if the local ordinance and the state statute conflict, then the state section governs and you should ask the judge that your ticket be dismissed.

After you've found the right law and derived the elements, you next want to get all the **evidence**. You can then **match** the evidence to the element(s) it tends to prove (evidence will often match more than one element in the government's case). This will not only organize the evidence, it will give you a clue as to how much evidence they have for each element, and suggest possible weaknesses in their case. We have here the first basis for *producing inconsistencies*.

Here's an example. Say you've been charged with driving without reasonable control, under §4511.202–TL. The prosecutor must prove, among other elements, that you were operating the vehicle on a street or highway or other public property. That's four separate elements: Who (you), doing what (operating), with what (a vehicle) and where (on a street or highway or other public property). Perhaps there was a witness who saw your vehicle driving…well, 'unreasonably.' Say she calls and then gives a written statement to the officer who arrives on the scene. She gets the license plate number correct, she identifies the vehicle to a tee (a blue nova with a 454 RAT), and she saw it on a particular street at a particular time. She also saw the driver, and identifies him on the written statement as a white male with brown hair, and notes a passenger. The police come to your door, and you say nothing, or if anything at all you deny everything, yet they issue you a citation, saying, "Well, it's my orders bud. I've gotta cite someone for something." You contact the witness, who you didn't know existed until you found out from the prosecutor. You're courteous, professional and sincere, *as always*. You talk and she tells you she made a statement to the police, and tells you generally what she told the officer.

***Very important note here. **Adults:** you don't necessarily have the right to get this prior statement from the prosecutor before trial! *See* Rule 16(B)(2)–CR. When you 'request discovery,' the prosecutor (often a legal intern) may still give you the prior statement in the report, not knowing, or not caring since it is 'just a traffic case.' More power to you. It doesn't hurt to request it. **Juveniles:** you *do* have the right to get this prior statement from the prosecutor. *See* Rule 24(A)(2)&(3)–JR. So you don't have to worry about asking the judge to see the written statement after she testifies, or anything like that. You'll be able to place the statement down on your desk and analyze it before trial. Sorry adults, but you've still got a chance because the prosecutor may give the written statement to you anyhow. Much more on this crucial topic in Chapter 5.

Anyhow, you're suspicious, so you match her statement with all four elements, since it tends to prove each. But you can also see where the weakness is, and it's a potentially *fatal* weakness. It doesn't seem she sufficiently identified who the operator was. If the prosecutor doesn't want to drop the case, you go to trial. At trial, the prosecutor asks and she points to you and says something like, "That's the guy." When the prosecutor is done questioning her, it's your turn (cross-examination). *For adults who didn't get the statement beforehand*: First, you request to the judge to see prior statements made by the witness: "Your honor, before questioning the witness, may I review all the prior statements she has made?" You, the judge and the prosecutor will go over this statement to see if there are any inconsistencies. You note the vague identification on the statement. The judge allows you to question on it. You arise slowly, and politely ask, "Ma'am, when the police officer arrived on the scene, you were honest with him, right?"

A. Of course I was.

Q. You, of course, told him everything that happened as accurately as you could?

A. Yes, as best I could.

Q. Because you wanted to help him in his investigation—help him catch the person who committed this crime, right?

A. Yes, I always do my best to help. (What a rube)

Q. And the officer took notes?

A. Yes.

Q. Ma'am, I couldn't help noticing as you just testified how sure you were it was me. You're sure it was me?

A. Definitely.

Q. You're very sure today—you were just as sure that afternoon, right?

A. Yes.

Q. Because you had just *witnessed* it?

A. Right, obviously.

Q. So, obviously, your recollection was fresher then?

A. Well, it's great right now too.

Q. Yes ma'am, but because you had just seen it happen, it was very fresh in your memory, right?

A. Uh, yeah. (She probably sees it coming now…too late)

Q. But you didn't identify me to the officer that afternoon, did you?

A. Yes I did.

Q. Your honor, I have the statement the witness made that afternoon to the police officer. (Let the prosecutor see it) May I approach the witness?

Judge. You may.

Q. Here's the statement you made to the officer that afternoon, ma'am. Look it over and tell us were you identified me.

A. Right here, I say a white male with brown hair.

Q. And nothing else?

A. (Looks it over) I guess not.

Q. Nothing about my freckles?

A. No.

Q. Nothing about my eyes?

A. No.

Q. Nothing about my small nose?

A. Well, I couldn't see *that* well.

Q. You only told the officer, "A white male with brown hair?"

A. Yes.

Q. Yet you're sure it was me?

A. Yes, I believe so.

Q. (Take the paper from her; go back to where you were standing) Even though all you saw was a white male with brown hair?

A. Well, no, that's not all I saw.

Q. What if I, or another witness, was to tell you I have a lot of friends, some of them white males with brown hair, who I let drive my vehicle. Could you, using your statement alone, distinguish us?

A. Well yes, it was you.

Q. Using only the statement ma'am?

A. Well, I didn't tell him *everything*, just what he needed to know to do his job. (Or something like this—they'll say it in an attempt to squirm out of saying, "No.")

Q. (This is why you asked the first questions) Ma'am, you just told me a moment ago that when the police officer arrived you told him everything you knew as accurately as possible, and to the best of your ability, and honestly—Now you're saying you *didn't*?!

It doesn't matter how she answers now. You've made your point. You can stop questioning her. The prosecution has trouble establishing identity, and they'll have to prove that it's your vehicle and only you had access to it (other elements they'll have to prove now, but probably didn't prepare to) in hopes that this will be sufficient to establish identity. In closing argument, you'll focus on this *inconsistency* that you've produced in their case. This alone is sufficient to establish a reasonable doubt. And it all happened because you discovered the **elements** the prosecution must prove beyond a reasonable doubt, you got your hands on the **evidence**, you **matched** the evidence to the elements, thereby noticing a weakness in their case, and developed questions to ask to draw this weakness out into an *inconsistency* at trial.

Notice particularly, you *didn't* do what other 'traffic defense' books instruct you to do: just wait until trial, "listen closely" to the testimony, take "scrupulous notes," and then try and think of something ingenious to ask the witness to destroy their case. My opinion of that method? One word: Bogus. Ridiculous. Won't work. To win, you've got to take action, pre-plan and prepare, and follow that plan completely unless something absolutely irresistible occurs (a flash of insight that reveals another inconsistency: *don't count on it*). The questions I asked? You've just got to think of your situation and the best questions to ask to get what you want—grounds for an inconsistency. I hope the examples throughout this book help you develop this technique. Note that you don't have to memorize all these questions, like some books advise. You can write or type them up, and use them in court this way, slowly, patiently and methodically asking each question. Just always be confident, professional and sincere. At the same time, keep incredulous.

So pay particular attention to this section, and the 'Procedures Section.' Your ability to *produce inconsistencies* in the government's case, which is your final result desired, depends almost entirely on the detail and accuracy of your efforts in applying these two sections. I've got to admit, it's all starting to make complete sense to me now.

5

Getting what they have

The way I see it, you all must be on the edge of your seats, waiting with bated breath to find out how to get the government's evidence against you. It's a very important chapter, so I'll go into detail with it. If you're a glutton, and want more detail, then there are numerous excellent textbooks about this subject at your local law library.

Discovery is the legal term for getting what they have and what you're allowed to get. As with all walks of life, information is the key to victory. They'll try to keep it; you should try to get it. Some of our better political representatives realized the advantages the government has in this contest, and so provided a legal mechanism (called discovery) to try and even out the score before the game begins. Truth is, though the representatives have done a fine job, the score still isn't square from the get-go, and the statutes need more work, the people need more leverage.

Keep in mind throughout this chapter that discovery is the statutory way of getting information for your case. You may also use traditional investigative tools, like going back and measuring the height of the speed sign, taking pictures, talking to witnesses, et cetera. To make your investigation as effective and fruitful as possible though, discovery is a must.

It potentially entails three documents: Notice Request, Discovery Request, Motion for Discovery.

After you get your ticket, the first time you'll go to court is called the arraignment. That's when you enter your plea. At the arraignment, or soon after practically speaking, you can request *notice* from the prosecuting attorney. *See* Rule 11(D)–TR. How? With a 'Notice Request' letter. Either hand it to him at the arraignment or mail it to him soon after. There's an example in the Appendix on Forms. What you're requesting is that the prosecutor gives you notice of his intention to use evidence at trial you're allowed to have access to before trial. Thus, for example, if the prosecution has any witnesses, they must now give you notice that they plan to use evidence at trial that you may discover (that is, that you're allowed to have access to before trial). If you don't give the letter, they are not obliged to give notice.

Once given notice, you may then make a 'Discovery Request.' *See* Rule 16–CR (for adults), Rule 24–JR (for juveniles). Make this request to the prosecutor. There's an example for each in the Appendix on Forms. Note: you don't have to make a *notice* request before making a *discovery* request; you can just skip the notice request if you like and just do a discovery request. It's the discovery request that gets you the evidence, such as the names and addresses of all witnesses and their prior felony record, documents and tangible objects, like photographs, documents or papers, that are material to the preparation of your defense, past statements made by you or a co-defendant, and evidence favorable to you and material to your guilt or punishment.

Finally, if the prosecutor denies your discovery request, or doesn't respond, then you can make a '*Motion* for Discovery.' Give this motion to *both* the prosecutor and the clerk of courts. There's an example in the Appendix on Forms. This is different from a request, being a bit more formal. You need to certify that the discovery request was made and that discovery was not provided. Note: In traffic cases, Motion's for Discovery are often made without *first* making a request. Though technically improper, it is generally accepted on efficiency grounds. When do you know you'll need to make this motion? Well, you must make a motion for discovery no later than twenty-one days after your arraignment, or seven days before your trial, whichever comes first.

First example: your trial is set for sixty days after your arraignment. You make a discovery *request* a few days after your arraignment. You wait a couple weeks, but no response. You'll need to get that *motion* out before twenty-one days has expired from your day of arraignment. Second example: your trial is set for only twenty-one days after your arraignment. You then will need to get your *motion* out in fourteen days (to meet the seven day requirement).

General method:

1   At the arraignment, give the prosecutor a Discovery Request, and have the judge record that it was delivered. Or if arraignment already occurred, mail the prosecutor a request as soon as you can. If you're not sure who to mail it to, call the clerk of courts, the number of whom should be on your ticket, and find out.

2   If the prosecutor denies or doesn't respond to the request, file a Motion for Discovery within the applicable timeframe, as noted above.

3   Note at your preliminary motions (*See* Practice Section, Preliminary Motions), before trial begins, that you did all of this, and request that a comparison be made with all evidence (documents, witnesses, et cetera) you received through discovery and all evidence the prosecutor plans on introducing at trial, asking for all evidence the prosecutor has that she didn't give to you, but was supposed to, be suppressed (not allow to be heard at trial).

If the prosecutor doesn't respond at all, or denies the request and motion? Well, they can potentially deny the request, but they can't *legally* deny an order from the court resulting from your motion (That's good old checks and balances acting up again; the judicial branch (judge) legally gives the executive branch (prosecutor) an order, and they must comply). During preliminary motions, you'll just show the judge the motion, the request, and the judge's record that it was delivered (may be a different judge), tell her nothing was received, and request that your case be dismissed for the prosecutor's failure to comply with the discovery rules, or, in the alternative, request that the judge suppress (not allow to be heard at the trial) all evidence that you should have been given access to but weren't: "Your honor, I gave the prosecutor both a discovery request, the delivery of which was acknowledged by the judge, and a motion for discovery (show the judge the paperwork). He didn't respond to any of these, as was his duty to do. Because of this, I request this case be dismissed, or at the very least this evidence be suppressed." Either way, you'll win. The judge, if she's completely batty, will deny your motion. Then you must ask for a continuance, "Your honor, I request a continuance for adequate time to receive this discovery and prepare my defense." If she's biased, then she'll deny this too. So say, "Your honor, I wish to preserve these motions on the record for purposes of appeal."

Do the same thing if they don't give you *all* the evidence they're supposed to. *See* number 3, above. For example, they call a witness at trial that they didn't give you the name of when you requested and received discovery. Object immediately. Stand and say, "Objection, your honor, the prosecution didn't inform me of this witness on discovery, and so he shouldn't be permitted to testify." Or they might try to introduce a prior written statement made by you, or maybe some photographs, that they didn't include when you requested and received discovery. Object as above, asking the judge to suppress the evidence. If the prosecutor *does* give you the appropriate information, but waits to the last second to do so, then ask the judge for a continuance, "Your honor, I request a continuance. Though I requested and motioned for discovery (show the judge the papers) within the proper timeframes, the prosecutor only gave me the information two days ago. As a result, I haven't had time to adequately prepare my defense, and so request a continuance."

So, that's it. That's how you get the proverbial **evidence** ball rolling. You've already got the ticket, which you'll analyze. Now you'll get the rest. What you'll do with this evidence is covered in the 'Producing Inconsistencies Section.'

Use similar techniques for attempting to get any and all important *procedures* that may be helpful to your case. *See* Procedures Section. Remember, not only does the prosecution have to prove the *elements* of the crime beyond a reasonable doubt, but also the law enforcement system in general has to follow certain *procedures* in order to enable your trial to occur in the first place. For example, say you were cited for speeding. Say the prosecutor has evidence that will prove all the elements of the law (§4511.21) beyond a reasonable doubt. He's then satisfied the *proof* requirement. But now assume that the speed limit sign on the street that you were pulled over on was improperly posted because, say, it didn't meet the Department of Transportation's height requirements. This is a *procedure* that the law enforcement division of the government must follow in order to legally enforce the speed limit against you. If you can show this procedure was not followed, even though all the so-called *material* elements are provable beyond a reasonable doubt, you'll have your case thrown out. *That's* the difference between proof and procedure, a crucial one, and that's why I emphasize their distinction by considering them in different sections.

6

The elements of identity and venue

No matter what they accuse you of, the government *must* show identity and venue. That is, they must offer evidence at trial to identify you as the person ticketed, and they must establish that *where* you were ticketed was in the jurisdiction of the court hearing your case (that's called venue: pronounced like 'thenyou,' but with a 'v' instead of a 'th,' got it? Some judges just call it *jurisdiction*, and that'll do too). If the government doesn't offer evidence to prove these elements then you must motion for a judgment of acquittal. It will be granted, your case will be dismissed, and you can shake the prosecutor's hand sincerely smiling. These two elements are then the first on your checklist.

How will they try to prove identity? Simple. When the officer takes the stand, the prosecutor will ask something like:

Q. On the morning of Jan10th, did you come into contact with someone you now know as John Doe (that's you)?

A. Yes.

Q. Do you see him in the courtroom today?

A. Yes.

Q. Please point him out and describe what he's wearing.

A. He's the young man sitting at the table there, wearing a tuxedo.

Then the prosecutor should say something like, "Your honor, may the record reflect that Officer Schmuckatelli has identified the defendant, John Doe?"

Judge. The record will so reflect.

Done.

If the prosecutor doesn't ask the judge the "may the record reflect" question, then you'll motion for judgment of acquittal at the appropriate time, and say, "Your honor, I motion for acquittal. The record doesn't reflect that I was identified." If the prosecutor doesn't cover these questions at all with any witness, then you'll definitely be granted your motion for acquittal.

How will they try to prove venue? Simple. The prosecutor will question the officer like this:

Q. Where did you come into contact with the defendant?

A. I pulled him over down on Valleydell Road.

Q. What County is Valleydell Road in?

A. It's here in Stark County?

Q. What city?

A. Well, it's *currently* part of Plain Township.

Done.

Not much for them to do to establish identity and venue. The police are given great discretion with identity, and venue is straightforward. But they must establish them nonetheless. Sometimes, a legal intern gets so involved with the substance of their case they forget these initial tasks. Have your checklist in front of you at trial, and if they don't cover these subjects, make a note of it. You'll be motioning for a judgment of acquittal based on these grounds. And if you're right, you'll win. The judge might even spare you the trouble and dismiss the case on his own.

7

Juvenile age and traffic court jurisdiction

For juveniles, the prosecutor must show that you were in fact a juvenile at the time of the traffic incident. This is straightforward too. Often, they'll just ask you to stipulate (agree) to the judge before trial that you in fact were a juvenile at the time of ticketing. Otherwise, they'll call a parent or guardian, who must be with you at trial, to testify as to your age on the date of the ticketing. If they ask you to stipulate, and you in fact were a juvenile at the time of the ticketing, then you might as well, since their asking pretty much means they've prepared the few questions they need to ask your parent/guardian to establish your age at the time…unless your parent is just dying to be a witness at a trial, which is okay too.

Secondly, and very importantly, on your ticket, the police *must* put, along with the purported violation, the statute number defining you as a juvenile traffic offender. This statute number is §2151.021–JCR. For instance, on the ticket, if they say you were speeding, you should see the numbers 4511.21 (speeding), *and* 2151.021. Often, the police forget to put 2151.021 on the ticket. Two scenarios result from this.

First, on trial-day or pre-trial day, during preliminary motions, the prosecutor will ask the magistrate to amend the ticket to include §2151.021. They'll say something like, "Your honor, the state motions to amend the ticket to include section 2151.021." The magistrate should ask if you have any objections to this. Even if he doesn't, you should object, stand and say, "May I object your honor—Your honor, the officer has the duty to fill out the citation completely. I showed him my identification that day, and he had ample opportunity to fill out the ticket properly and completely. He should not be allowed to sidestep that duty." Remember; *always* be sincere, professional, confident and respectful to the court (and in court). Depending on the magistrate, the ruling could go either way. If you're respectful, sincere and professional, and the magistrate has half a heart, he just may grant it. It's worth the try. If it works, your case will be dismissed.

What else might happen? The prosecutor might fail to notice that 2151.021 wasn't written on the ticket. Then what happens? Well, after the prosecutor is done her side of the case and says, "The state rests," it will be your turn. And you'll immediately ask the magistrate to dismiss the case, stand and say, "Your honor, I request dismissal of this case. The state failed to include the required statute, section 2151.021, to establish jurisdiction over me as a juvenile traffic offender." Or the court, on its own motion (they can do that), may dismiss.

8

The traffic law they claim you violated

First of all, read your ticket: the whole thing, including the back. Where will you find what law you were cited under? On the front part of your ticket, in the boxes with "ORC, ORD, TP" in them, is where the number of the statute (law) usually is. If there isn't a statute number written anywhere on the ticket, see Chapter 15.

Here are important parts of a number of the more common traffic laws the police use when issuing citations. Also, under each law you'll find the elements the government must show to prove you guilty (though identity, venue and juvenile age are not necessarily so-called *material* elements of each law, I include them anyway because the government must show them). If you think you see another element that the prosecution must prove, and that I haven't included in my list of elements, by all means go for it. I don't proclaim to have deciphered these laws perfectly. My effort is to create a target for you to shoot your arrows at. You may find other targets. If you're ever unsure or think you're onto something, search out the actual statute at the local law library. *See* Appendix, Helpful Contacts.

§4511.13(C)(1) (Red light)

Vehicular traffic, streetcars, and trackless trolleys facing a steady red signal alone shall stop at a clearly marked stop line, but if none, before entering the crosswalk on the near side of the intersection, or if none, then before entering the intersection and shall remain standing until an indication to proceed is shown...

Elements:

(1) Identity

(2) Venue

(3) Age (juveniles)

(4) Facing a steady red signal

(5) Failed to stop

(6) At a clearly marked stop line

(7) (If there isn't a clearly marked stop line) Before entering the crosswalk

(8) (If there isn't this either) Before entering the intersection.

§4511.15(A)&(B) (Flashing red light and Flashing yellow light)

(A) Flashing red stop signal: Operators of vehicles, trackless trolleys, and streetcars shall stop at a clearly marked stop line, but if none, before entering the crosswalk on the near side of the intersection, or if none, then at the point nearest the intersection roadway where the driver has a view of approaching traffic on the intersecting roadway before entering it, and the right to proceed shall be subject to the rules applicable after making a stop at a stop sign.

(B) Flashing yellow caution signal: Operators of vehicles, trackless trolleys, and streetcars may proceed through the intersection or past such signal only with caution.

Elements:

(1) Identity

(2) Venue

(3) Age (juveniles)

(4) Failed to stop

(5) At a clearly marked stop line

(6) (If there isn't a clearly marked stop line) Before entering crosswalk

(7) (If there isn't this either) At a point nearest the intersection where you have a view

(8) Must yield right-of-way (see definition in §4511.41) as if you're stopped at a stop sign

(9) Yellow light: proceed only with caution.

§4511.20 (Reckless operation)

No person shall operate a vehicle, trackless trolley, or streetcar on any street or highway in willful or wanton disregard of the safety of persons or property.

Elements:

(1) Identity

(2) Venue

(3) Age (juveniles)

(4) Operate

(5) A motor vehicle

(6) On a street or highway

(7) Willful or wanton disregard of the safety of persons/property.

§4511.201 (Reckless operation *off* streets and highways)

No person shall operate a vehicle, trackless trolley, or streetcar on any public or private property other than streets or highways, in willful or wanton disregard of the safety of persons or property.

This section does not apply to the competitive operation of vehicles on public or private property when the owner of such property knowingly permits such operation thereon.

Elements:

(1) Identity

(2) Venue

(3) Age (juveniles)

(4) Operate

(5) A motor vehicle

(6) On public or private property *other than* streets or highways

(7) Willful or wanton disregard of the safety of persons/property.

§4511.202 (Operating without reasonable control)

No person shall operate a motor vehicle, trackless trolley, or streetcar on any street, highway, or property open to the public for vehicular traffic without being in reasonable control of the vehicle, trolley, or streetcar.

Elements:

(1) Identity

(2) Venue

(3) Age (juveniles)

(4) Operate

(5)   A motor vehicle

(6)   On a street, highway or any property open to the public for vehicular traffic

(7)   Without reasonable control of the vehicle.

§4511.21 (Speed limits and Assured clear distance)

This section is expansive, and I'm a lowsy typist, so I quote only parts of sections here that the police usually cite under and that will be important for our analysis in the 'Producing Inconsistencies Section.'

(A)   No person shall operate a motor vehicle, trackless trolley, or streetcar at a speed greater or less than is reasonable or proper, having due regard to the traffic, surface, and width of the street or highway and any other conditions, and no person shall drive any motor vehicle, trackless trolley, or streetcar in and upon any street or highway at a greater speed than will permit the person to bring it to a stop within the assured clear distance ahead.

(B)   It is prima facie lawful…(various)

(C)   It is prima facie unlawful…(various)

I bet you're asking, "What the heck does prima facie mean?" Well, it turns out this will be a very important term when it comes to defending your speeding ticket. No kidding. You'll be amazed at the defenses that arise because of it being a part of Ohio traffic law. It's pronounced prime-uh fâ-she. Lawyers pronounce it other ways too, just to sound intellectual and all. For our purposes here, it means *presumed*. For example, if you're caught driving 35mph in a 25mph speed zone, then it is *presumed* to be unlawful. You could say, it is *presumed* unlawful—or you could say, it is *prima facie* unlawful. You might be asking what the big deal is about all this prima facie stuff. "If I'm speeding, I'm speeding.

It doesn't matter if it's prima facie speeding, prima donna (yes, for this term the word prima is pronounced premuh—go figure Latin) speeding, or just plain, good old-fashioned petal to the metal rollin'." Well, okay, but if you think about it, what it means is that it's only *presumed* that your driving is unlawful. You could actually be driving 35mph in a 25mph, and in fact be driving *lawfully*.

No kidding. Doesn't matter what the radar, laser or VASCAR said. The vast majority of Ohio drivers don't know this, but it's the dead truth. I'll go into this subject in detail in the 'Producing Inconsistencies Section,' when I cover speeding. But since you brought it up, I'll tell you this: If you can show that, *despite* driving over the posted speed limit, you were driving *reasonably under the conditions*, then your ticket will be dismissed…Yep, no kidding.

Elements (Assured clear distance):

(1)   Identity

(2)   Venue

(3)   Age (juveniles)

(4)   Drive

(5)   A motor vehicle

(6)   On a street or highway

(7)   At a greater speed than will permit you to bring it to a stop within the assured clear distance.

§4511.251 (Street racing)

(A)   [Street racing] means the operation of two or more vehicles from a point side by side at accelerating speeds in a competitive attempt to out-distance each other or the operation of one or more vehicles over a common selected course, from the same point to the same point, wherein timing is made of the participating vehicles involving competitive accelerations or speeds. Person rendering assistance in any manner to such competitive use of vehicles shall be equally charged as the participants. The operation of two or more vehicles side by side either at speeds in excess of prima facie lawful speeds or rapidly accelerating from a common starting point to a speed in excess of such prima facie lawful speeds shall be prima facie evidence of street racing.

(B)   No person shall participate in street racing upon any public road, street, or highway in this state.

Elements:

(1)   Identity

(2)   Venue

(3)   Age (juveniles)

(4)   Participation in

(5)   Operating

(6)   Two or more vehicles

(7)   From a point side-by-side

(8)   At accelerating speeds

(9)   Must be a competitive attempt to out-distance each other, *or*

(10) Operating

(11) One or more vehicles

(12) Over a course

(13) The course must be common and selected

(14) From the same point to the same point

(15) Timing is made of the vehicles.

Note the prima facie rule in the last sentence. It will be important later. For a definition of prima facie, see §4511.21's discussion.

§4511.33 (Driving in marked lanes)

(A) A vehicle or trackless trolley shall be driven, as nearly as is practicable, entirely within a single lane or line of traffic and shall not be moved from such lane or line until the driver has first ascertained that such movement can be made with safety.

Elements:

(1) Identity

(2) Venue

(3) Age (juveniles)

(4) Vehicle moved from lane

(5) Before driver ascertained that such move

(6) Can be made with safety.

§4511.41 (Right-of-way at intersections)

(A) When two vehicles, including any trackless trolley or streetcar, approach or enter an intersection from different streets or highways at approximately the same time, the driver of the vehicle on the left shall yield the right-of-way to the vehicle on the right.

Right-of-way means: The right of a vehicle, streetcar, trackless trolley, or pedestrian to proceed uninterruptedly in a *lawful* manner in the direction in which it or the individual is moving in preference to another vehicle, streetcar, trackless trolley, or pedestrian approaching from a different direction into its or the individual's path.

Note: In the statutes, the right-of-way of a driver is *presumed* (the prosecutor doesn't have to prove it). For example, for this law, the prosecutor only has to show that your vehicle was indeed "on the left." Once they've done this, the right-of-way of the other vehicle is presumed, and you'll have to offer evidence to show otherwise.

Nonetheless, the government must still prove your *failure to yield* this right-of-way. Some people argue about what is necessary to establish the failure to yield element. Some say, absent evidence to the contrary, if there is an accident and the other driver had the right-of-way, the accident itself will be sufficient to establish that you failed to yield this right-of-way. Others say hogwash. What do I say? Hell, argue every point you can and let the judge sort it out.

Elements:

(1)   Identity

(2)   Venue

(3)   Age (juveniles)

(4)   Driver

(5)   Of a vehicle on the left

(6)   Failed to yield right-of-way.

§4511.39 (Turn signals)

No person shall turn a vehicle or trackless trolley or move right or left upon a highway unless and until such person has exercised due care to ascertain that the movement can be made with reasonable safety nor without giving an appropriate signal in the manner hereinafter provided.

When required, a signal of intention to turn or move right or left shall be given continuously during not less than the last one hundred feet traveled by the vehicle or trackless trolley before turning.

I included §4511.39 because it will be used in the 'Producing Inconsistencies Section.'

§4511.42 (Right-of-way when turning left)

The operator of a vehicle, streetcar, or trackless trolley intending to turn to the left within an intersection or into an alley, private road, or driveway shall yield the right-of-way to any vehicle, streetcar, or trackless trolley approaching from the opposite direction, whenever the approaching vehicle, streetcar, or trackless trolley is within the intersection or so close to the intersection, alley, private road, or driveway as to constitute an immediate hazard.

Elements:

(1)   Identity

(2)   Venue

(3)   Age (juveniles)

(4)   Operating

(5)   A motor vehicle

(6)   With intent to turn left

(7)   You're within an intersection, or

(8)   Intend to turn left into an alley, etc.

(9)   Failure to yield right-of-way

(10) To a vehicle approaching from the opposite direction

(11) When that vehicle is within the intersection, or

(12) So close to the intersection as to constitute an immediate hazard.

§4511.43 (Right-of-way at through highways, stop and yield signs)

(A) Except when directed to proceed by a law enforcement officer, every driver of a vehicle or trackless trolley approaching a stop sign shall stop at a clearly marked stop line, but if none, before entering the crosswalk on the near side of the intersection, or, if none, then at the point nearest the intersecting roadway where the driver has a view of approaching traffic on the intersecting roadway before entering it. After having stopped, the driver shall yield the right-of-way to any vehicle in the intersection or approaching on another roadway so closely as to constitute an immediate hazard during the time the driver is moving across or within the intersection or junction or roadways.

(B) The driver of a vehicle or trackless trolley approaching a yield sign shall slow down to a speed reasonable for the existing conditions and, if required for safety to stop, shall stop at a clearly marked stop line, but if none, before entering the crosswalk on the near side of the intersection, or, if none, then at the point nearest the intersecting roadway where the driver has a view of approaching traffic on the intersecting roadway before entering it. After slowing or stopping, the driver shall yield the right-of-way to any vehicle or trackless trolley in the intersection or approaching on another roadway so closely as to constitute an immediate hazard during the time the driver is moving across or within the intersection or junction of roadways.

Whenever a driver is involved in a collision with a vehicle or trackless trolley in the intersection or junction of roadways, after driving past a yield sign without stopping, the collision shall be prima facie evidence of the driver's failure to yield the right-of-way.

Elements (Stop sign):

(1)   Identity

(2)   Venue

(3)   Age (juveniles)

(4)   Driver

(5)   Of a motor vehicle

(6)   Approaching a stop sign

(7)   Failed to stop

(8)   At a clearly marked stop line

(9)   (If there is no clearly marked stop line) Before entering the crosswalk

(10) (Of there isn't this either) At the point nearest the intersection where you have a view of approaching traffic on the intersecting roadway

(11) After stopping, failed to yield right-of-way

(12) To a vehicle in the intersection, *or*

(13) To a vehicle in the intersection or approaching *on another roadway* so closely as to constitute an *immediate* hazard.

Elements (Yield sign):

(1)   Approaching a yield sign

(2)   Failed to slow down to a reasonable speed for the existing conditions, and

(3)   If required for safety to stop, failed to stop

(4)   At a clearly marked stop line

(5)   (If there is no clearly marked stop line) Before entering the crosswalk

(6) (If there isn't this either) At the point nearest the intersecting roadway where you have a view of approaching traffic on the intersecting roadway

(7) After slowing or stopping, failed to yield right-of-way

(8) To a vehicle in the intersection, *or*

(9) To a vehicle approaching *on another roadway* so closely as to constitute an *immediate* hazard.

Note the prima facie rule in the last sentence of the rule. It will be important later. For one definition and the pronunciation of prima facie, see §4511.21's discussion. Here though, "prima facie evidence of" is used to mean 'sufficient to prove the element beyond a reasonable doubt.' That is, the collision shall be 'sufficient to prove beyond a reasonable doubt' the driver's failure to yield the right-of way. But the prosecution will first have to show that you drove past the yield sign without stopping.

§4511.75(A) (Stopping for a school bus)

The driver of a vehicle, streetcar, or trackless trolley upon meeting or overtaking from either direction any school bus stopped for the purpose of receiving or discharging any school child, person attending programs offered by community boards of mental health and county boards of mental retardation and developmental disabilities, or child attending a program offered by a head start agency, shall stop at least ten feet from the front or rear of the school bus and shall not proceed until such school bus resumes motion, or until signaled by the school bus driver to proceed.

It is not defense to a charge under this division that the school bus involved failed to display or be equipped with an automatically extended stop warning sign as required by division (B) of this section.

Elements:

(1) Identity

(2) Venue

(3) Age (juveniles)

(4) Driver

(5) Of a motor vehicle

(6) Meeting or overtaking a school bus

(7) School bus must be stopped for the purpose described

(8) Failed to stop

(9) At least ten feet from the front or rear

(10) Proceeded before school bus resumed motion, *or*

(11) Before signaled by the school bus driver to proceed.

Section Three

Procedures

9

To begin with

This section covers various procedures (regulations) the law enforcement division, and in general the executive branch of government (including the prosecutor) which law enforcement is a part, must follow in order to legally enforce your purported violation. The legislative branch, for instance the Ohio General Assembly, creates some of these procedures. The executive branch, for instance the Department of Transportation (DOT), pursuant to powers given them by the legislative branch, creates others. I also suggest ways to find out if these procedures have been followed.

You should make a checklist of all the procedures you find that the government must follow. There's a checklist example in the Appendix on Forms. After you've done this, you can go about seeing if they've abided by them. In this section, I cover a number of the more interesting and promising types of procedures and regulations. They may prove good grounds for producing inconsistencies in the government's case against you. In fact, many of these procedures are deemed so important that your case will be dismissed before it even begins if you find that they haven't been followed. An example is the engineering and traffic investigation that local authorities or board of township trustees must do to change a prima facie speed limit. For a definition and discussion of the term 'prima facie,' see Section II, Chapter 8's discussion of §4511.21 (speed limits).

10

Tickets based on traffic signs, the OMUTCD and E&T studies

This chapter is a *must read*. Though focusing on Ohio law, it will provide numerous ideas for readers from other states.

Traffic signs fall under the legal lingo of "traffic control devices." *See* §4511.01(QQ)–TL. To be a legal, official traffic control device, a sign must meet certain requirements. If the sign doesn't, then it's not official and it can't be enforced against you. Recall the forty roads in Plain Township spoken of in the preface, which were improperly posted for over forty years. This should give you a feel for how important this section is and how the government violates these various regulations.

First understand, roads have presumed (lawyers call them prima facie) speeds on them. Even if a road doesn't have a speed limit sign posted, these prima facie speeds are in effect. For instance, the prima facie speed on highways outside municipal corporations is fifty-five, with one exception. Here's the trick though. If the local authorities or board of township trustees want to *change* this prima facie speed limit, for instance, because the speed is too high for the conditions, they can. But they can *only* do this if they follow certain regulations (laws). Otherwise, the speed limits aren't *really* changed, no matter that there are speed limit signs posted. In the above example, the board of township trustees could change the prima facie speed from fifty-five to, say, thirty-five, but if they didn't follow the proper regulations then all those 35mph speed limit signs are bogus and illegal, they have to be taken down, and the real speed limit never changed, remaining 55mph all the while. So if you were ticketed for going 47mph in that zone, then your ticket will be thrown out, because you weren't really exceeding the *legal* speed limit. In fact, if you were ticketed for going 66mph in that zone, then your ticket should still be thrown out because you were potentially cited under the wrong law. But all this will occur and your ticket will be thrown out *only if* you make the effort to discover this governmental indiscretion and point it out. How did the Plain Township officials violate the statutes, and how does this help you?

Engineering and traffic investigation

To change a prima facie speed limit (See §4511.21 analysis, Chapter 8, for definition and discussion of prima facie), local authorities or the board of township trustees must first do an engineering and traffic (E&T) investigation justifying and legalizing their resolution. This is what they didn't do on those 40 Plain Township roads. There are also provisions for the interstate system. *See* §4511.21(L)&(M). Here's some of the applicable language (italics added).

§4511.21(I)(1)

…[W]henever *local authorities* determine *upon the basis of* an engineering and traffic investigation that the speed permitted by divisions (B)(1)(a) to (D) of this section, on any part of a highway under their jurisdiction, is greater than is reasonable and safe under the conditions found to exist at such location, the local authorities may by *resolution request the director* to determine and declare a reasonable and safe prima facie speed limit. Upon receipt of such request the director *may* determine and declare a reasonable and safe prima facie speed limit at such location…[S]uch declared speed limit shall become *effective only when appropriate* signs giving notice thereof are erected at such location by the local authorities.

§4511.21(K)(5)(b)¶2

Whenever a *board of township trustees* finds upon the basis of an engineering and traffic investigation that the prima facie speed permitted by division (B)(5) (55mph on highways outside municipal corporations other than freeways as provided by (B)(12)) of this section on any part of a highway under its jurisdiction that is located in a commercial or residential subdivision…is greater than is reasonable and safe under the conditions found to exist at the location, the board may by resolution declare a reasonable and safe prima facie speed limit of less than fifty-five by not less than twenty-five miles per hour at the location. An altered speed limit adopted…under this division…shall become effective when appropriate signs giving notice thereof are erected at the location by the township.

§4511.12¶1

No…driver of a vehicle…shall disobey the instructions of any traffic control device *placed in accordance with* this chapter…

§4511.12¶2

No provision of this chapter for which signs are required *shall be enforced* against an *alleged* violator if at the time and place of the alleged violation an *official* sign is not in…position…

What all of this means is that the road you were ticketed on may have required an E&T investigation for its posted speed limit. *Section 4511.21(B)* gives the prima facie speed limit on the road you were traveling on *in the absence of* a resolution pursuant to an engineering and traffic investigation changing it. For example, §4511.21(B)(5) provides in part:

> It is prima facie lawful, in the absence of a lower limit declared pursuant to this section by the director or transportation or local authorities, for the operator of a motor vehicle…to operate the same at a speed not exceeding…fifty-five miles per hour on highways outside municipal corporations…

If an E&T investigation was required, find out if one was done, if a resolution was made, and if the DOT accepted the resolution. How?

(1) Get in touch with the county or township engineer (Look in the blue pages of the phone book or get the number on the net). Or, if the road is in, say, Plain Township, get in touch with the township engineer…go to one of their bimonthly meetings or call. Ask: "Ma'am/Sir, I wanted to know if XYZ road had an engineering and traffic investigation done on it to approve its speed signs, if there was a resolution, and if the department of transportation accepted it. If so, can I get a copy of the paperwork?" Go down there and ask.

(2) You can also request it from the prosecutor as part of discovery. *See* Appendix on Forms, Discovery Request, E&T, followed up by a Motion for Discovery if necessary.

Just specify in the request that you want to see the engineering and traffic investigation and all other related papers, such as the resolution requesting or establishing the speed limit and the DOT's acceptance of this resolution and declaration of the new speed limit. **It's not clear if they're *required* to actually get the documents for you, and if so which ones.**

(3) Or you can request that the prosecutor present it to you *at trial.* *See* Appendix on Forms, E&T Production. This will at least get them looking into it. Thing is, then you won't know if the E&T investigation was done until trial, and if the prosecutor 'forgets' to bring it, then it's not entirely clear what a judge or magistrate might do when you object: "Your honor, I requested that the prosecutor bring the applicable engineering and traffic investigation as well as the resolutions and the department of transportation's acceptance to court (show judge the request). He's failed to do this your honor, and so I request a dismissal of my ticket." [Cold-hearted judge], "Denied." You, "Well, can I at least have a continuance to prepare my defense?" [Warm-hearted judge] (reads documents), "Ma'am/Sir, you've raised a very interesting point," to prosecutor, "Is this true?"

Prosecutor, "Uhhh."

Judge, "Case dismissed."

You, "Thank you, your honor."

What if you find out that the speed limit posted required an E&T investigation, but one was never done? Or having been done, a resolution was never adopted, or the DOT, if required or requested to, never accepted this resolution? Or perhaps some or all of this was done *after* you were cited. Then file a motion to dismiss immediately. *See* Appendix on Forms, Motion to Dismiss, E&T. Give the motion to the clerk of courts and the prosecutor. Who and where is the clerk of courts? Call the prosecutor; look in the blue pages. Ask around. Once you give them this, keep on top of it. Call the clerk of courts and the prosecutor and ask the status of your motion. Always be professional. If you're right about it, you'll win.

Who does the Engineering and traffic investigation

Who does the E&T investigation is just as important as how it's done. The Ohio Attorney General (OAG) has said that a board of township trustees may *not* contract out for the services of a professional traffic engineer to conduct the E&T investigation required under §4511.21(K) above, instead of having the *county engineer* conduct the investigation. *See* OAG 89–011 (Ask the law librarian to help you find this). Makes sense, why have a county engineer? Thus, if a board of township trustees did everything else properly, but contracted out to have the E&T investigation done, then the speed limit is invalid and cannot be enforced against you. Motion to dismiss on these grounds. For instance, Jackson Township, Ohio, contracted out with M-E Companies, a private engineering firm, for $5,000 to do an E&T investigation to lower the speed limits on stretches of Amherst Avenue NW, Promway Avenue NW and Mudbrook Street NW.[8] *But that's what the county engineer is getting paid to do*! So, according to the OAG, this is not allowed, and the speed changes are invalid. They're all *still* 55mph speed zones, as they were before. If you were ticketed for going say, 55mph on Amherst (which they changed to 45mph), then you're not guilty. You can motion to dismiss—Even if you were going *over* 55mph because you were probably cited under the wrong statutory section.

Another great instance is Plain Township, Ohio, which contracted out with M-E Companies to do the E&T investigation for Firestone Road NE.[9] Said an M-E agent, "for the most part (Ohio Department of Transportation officials) take what we recommend." They recommended that all studied portions be set at 30mph. Unfortunately, according to OAG 89–011 what M-E Companies recommends is of no legal weight. The speed limit on Firestone Road NE is *still* 55mph. It doesn't matter what the signs say; they're unofficial because they weren't posted pursuant to an E&T investigation done by the *county engineer*, which the Ohio Attorney General requires. If you were given a ticket for going, say, 53mph in the posted 30 or 35mph speed zone, then you're not guilty. The proper action would be to motion to dismiss. This is not a mere technicality. It is the law—Period. *You* pay the county engineer; *s/he* does the E&T investigation.

You can only *imagine* how many speed signs out there, cemented into the ground and bellowing out their speed limits, **are actually unofficial,** invalid, and so unenforceable (their bellows are but a whimper), because the E&T investigation was contracted out.

Also note that a board of township trustees may *not* contract out for the services of a professional traffic engineer to obtain a recommendation about the desirability of a township *road regulation* under §4511.21(I), instead of having the county or township engineer conduct the investigation. *See* OAG 89–011. Thus, if you find that the board of trustees relied on a professional traffic engineer's recommendation (instead of their county engineer's) in establishing *other types of road regulations* (besides speed limits) under §4511.21(I), that you were ticketed for allegedly violating, then you can motion to dismiss on these grounds. So, for instance, if they decided to put a yield sign in based on a professional traffic engineer's recommendation, and you were ticketed because of an alleged violation of this yield sign, you can motion to dismiss based on these grounds.

It seems like a complex topic, especially when you read the statutes. The parts I put in here are just that, parts! But the idea is simple: local government isn't allowed to arbitrarily make and enforce speed limits or other road regulations. Law enforcement, and the executive branch in general, must abide by certain regulations that the legislative branch has established. If they don't, they're breaking the law. It's the good old checks and balances at play, and it's a beautiful thing. It's the American way. Other aspects of the E&T investigation are considered in the next section on the Ohio Manual of Uniform Traffic Control Devices.

Ohio Manual of Uniform Traffic Control Devices (OMUTCD)

The OMUTCD is an excellent manual, prepared under the auspices of the Ohio Department of Transportation. The engineers and others who developed, contributed to and authored this manual did a class job. The OMUTCD clearly and distinctly points out what law enforcement and local authorities must or may do to establish and enforce traffic rules. It covers everything from traffic sign placement and dimensions to traffic signal heights to special signs for construction areas to placement of guide signs. They also provide the *policies* behind the various regulations, from public safety to driver notice. That being the case, you should refer to it. Your local law library should have a copy, or your county/township engineer will too. *See* Appendix, Helpful Contacts.

That being said, keep in mind that a board of township trustees can only change the speed on certain *residential* type streets. The OMUTCD provides that the E&T investigation should include an evaluation of the area to ensure that it meets the requirements of a "residential subdivision." *See* OMUTCD, §5D–7(Rev. 20); §4511.21(K)(5)(b). So check the E&T investigation paperwork to see if this was done. If not, you have grounds for filing a motion for dismissal. This is one of the reasons it's a very good idea to get this paperwork before trial, so that you can investigate completely and perhaps avoid trial all together.

The OMUTCD further provides that the E&T investigation *should* include documentation of the *terminal points* and approximate length of the proposed speed zone. It turns out that these terminal points may in fact be *required*. That's because the OMUTCD also says that a "Speed Zone cannot be enforced until…the first Speed Limit sign in each Speed Zone and first sign indicating the legal speed beyond the Speed Zone *shall* be located at the terminal points." *See* OMUTCD, §5D–10(Rev. 20, italics added). What's more, "the last sign in the zone shall display the legal speed limit of the road ahead." *See* §5D–10. Either the E&T investigation must include these terminal points, or some other public document that the people can review must. So if there's a 100yd Speed Zone of 25mph established by an E&T investigation, and immediately after this Speed Zone the speed changes to, say, 45mph, then the 0yd marker and the 100yd marker serve as the 'terminal points' of the Speed Zone.

Now, this 25mph Speed Zone *cannot be enforced* unless, among other things, there's a 25mph speed limit sign at the 0yd marker *and* a 45mph speed limit sign at the 100yd marker (going that direction). You could've been going 47mph in the Zone, but if they don't have a 45mph speed limit sign posted at the 100yd marker terminal point, which is identified in the E&T investigation, then the 25mph speed zone is unenforceable. You can motion to dismiss on these grounds. Keep in mind, that this 'terminal points condition' must be satisfied in *both directions* on the roadway you were ticketed on for it to be an enforceable speed zone in either direction.

Other OMUTCD provisions

Here are some *more* good old checks and balances, courtesy of the OMUTCD. Read the following laws first, and then we'll go into some specific examples (italics added).

§4511.09

The department of transportation shall adopt a manual and specifications for a uniform system of traffic control devices...

§4511.10¶1

The department of transportation may place and maintain traffic control devices, conforming to its manual and specifications...

§4511.11(A)

Local authorities in their respective jurisdictions *shall* place and maintain traffic control devices in accordance with the department of transportation manual and specifications for a uniform system of traffic control devices...

§4511.11(D)

All traffic control devices erected on a public road, street, or alley, shall conform to the state manual and specifications.

§4511.12¶2

No provision of this chapter for which signs are required *shall be enforced* against an *alleged* violator if at the time and place of the alleged violation an *official* sign is not in proper position and sufficiently legible to be seen by an ordinarily observant person. Whenever a particular section of this chapter does not state that signs are required, that section shall be effective even though no signs are erected or in place.

If the law you were cited under concerned a sign, and the sign didn't meet OMUTCD requirements at the time of your citation, then the sign was not official and the law can't be enforced against you. If it's an official sign, but it's not in proper position *and* sufficiently legible, then it can't be enforced against you either. I must say this, don't ever claim that the OMUTCD requirements for a sign haven't been met, then take the stand (testify) and admit *seeing* the sign. The Ohio Supreme Court has held: "It would be an anomalous situation if one approaching a traffic signal could say, 'that signal is not erected strictly in conformity with the requirements of the statute and the traffic ordinance and, therefore, I can disregard it.'" *See* Mansfield v. Carman, 159 Ohio St. 558 (This notation means: 159 is the volume, Ohio St. is the book, 558 is the page number. The law librarian can help you with this). At the same time, *never* take the stand and lie. Just don't take the stand. It's your constitutional right not to have to. Either way, if you find that the sign didn't meet OMUTCD requirements, you can immediately file a motion to dismiss, and so hopefully won't get to the trial stage.

First off, how do you get access to the OMUTCD? You can talk to your county or township engineer. They have copies. There are also law libraries across the state with the OMUTCD on shelf. *See* Appendix, Helpful Contacts. For instance, there's an excellent law library in the Central Plaza building where the Stark County prosecutor's office is that has a copy. The law library personnel are very helpful and an excellent resource. You can also go to a law school's library. If they don't have it, they have computer accounts showing which law libraries do. Finally, there are numerous internet sites on the OMUTCD. See Appendix, Helpful Contacts.

What do you do if you find out the sign didn't meet the OMUTCD requirements? Just as with the E&T investigation, you would file a motion to dismiss. Or bring it up in your preliminary motions on trial day. Show evidence of it: a picture, a witness (other than yourself), other documentation, et cetera.

Here are some examples of OMUTCD requirements. When I cite to the OMUTCD below, it will be to the section and the twentieth revision, thus: *See* 5D–1 means *See* OMUTCD, §5D–1(Rev. 20).

Speed Zones

"A Speed Zone cannot be enforced until standard signs have been properly installed along the roadway." *See* 5D–10. This includes the terminal points discussion, above. It also requires that speed limit signs be posted (1) just beyond each point where traffic enters the street or highway from other major public roadways or major access points, *and* (2) at intervals throughout the zone. *See* 5D–10. Check each of these requirements out too. If one of them is not met, then "standard signs" haven't "been properly installed along the roadway," and the "Speed Zone cannot be enforced." You know the word: Motion to Dismiss!

Traffic Signs

Height

Sign height standards are often violated. Section 2E–4 covers the general topic. It also provides excellent illustrations. In *rural* districts, signs must be mounted at a height of *at least* 5 feet. This measurement is made from the bottom of the sign straight down to the level of the near edge of pavement. If it doesn't meet this standard, as all the others, the sign isn't official, and so it's enforceability is kaput.

***Very importantly**, and usually the case, in business, commercial or residential districts, "where parking and/or pedestrian movement is likely to occur or where there are other obstructions to view," the height of the sign must be *at least 7 feet*. If you look at the OMUTCD illustration, you'll see that if there is a *curb*, and the road sits below this curb (as is the norm in business, commercial or residential areas), the height is *not* measured to the level of the *road*. It is measured from the bottom of the sign to the point level with the top of the curb (thus, from the bottom of the sign straight down to the *top* of the curb). This is a good thing, because otherwise there's an additional, say, 6-10 inches (the height of a curb) that is added to the height of the sign.

So, for example, if the sign is posted next to a sidewalk near a donut shop, or if its posted next to a fair grounds (or any other area or *district* where parking and/or pedestrian movement is likely to occur), then the sign must be at least 7 feet high. Or, say, there are bushes or shrubs or a pack of lawyers standing around (or any other type of obstruction to view), then the sign must be at least 7 feet high. That simple; otherwise enforceability is kaput. One word: Motion to Dismiss. Ever seen those stop signs in shopping mall through-roads that are about one foot off the ground? Strictly for the birds.

Dimensions

Sign dimensions are required to be standard, though *increases* above the standard sizes are legitimate if greater legibility or emphasis is needed. *See* 2C–5. For example, the standard dimensions for stop signs is 30"x30". Perhaps you have seen those miniature stop signs around that have dimensions like 15"x15"? These are unofficial traffic control devices.

Lettering

Sign lettering must be in upper-case letters. *See* 2C–8. If they mess this one up, vote for someone else next time.

Borders

The corners of the borders or outlines of a sign must be rounded. *See* 2C–9. No kidding, and by 'corners of borders or outlines' they *don't* mean the corners of the sign panel itself (what we laypeople might call the *sign*, you know). No kidding. The OMUTCD gives illustrations showing what borders or outlines mean. A border is always inside a margin. It's like the white border inside the red margin on the combination speed/yield/stop/caution sign on the cover page. That's an example of a *border*. Notice it's not rounded at the corners, so it doesn't conform to the OMUTCD. Otherwise, I think it's okay…at least that's what some local law enforcement officials have told me during one of their breaks. Regardless, One word.

Illumination or reflectorization

In the wacky world of OMUTCD, reflectorization is classified as a *real* word. So is *'reflectorized.'* All signs, unless specifically provided for otherwise, must be 'reflectorized' or illuminated to show the same shape and color both by day and night. *See* 2D–1. Street or highway lighting *doesn't* satisfy this requirement. Illumination may be satisfied by means of a light behind the signs face, an attached or independently mounted light source designed for this purpose, or "some other effective device," such as luminous tubing. *See* 2D–2. Reflectorization may be satisfied by means of reflector buttons set into the sign, or with a material that has a "smooth, sealed outer surface," on the signs background or possibly in the message and border. *See* 2D–3.

Location

Generally, signs should be located on the right. For stop signs, for example, one *must* be. *See* 2H–5. Furthermore, for stop and yield signs, they must be placed at or as near as possible to the point where they want you to stop your car. Any stop *line* is merely *supplemental. See* 2H–5. So if an officer testifies and says you didn't stop at the stop *line*, but crossed over it and only stopped afterwards, and you take a picture showing the stop line is well *behind* the stop sign, then you've got a case that, okay, you may have not stopped at the stop *line* but you did stop at the point designated by the stop *sign*. Driving in town, you'll see this exact situation just dying to be litigated.

Lateral Clearance

Finally, signs normally should not be closer than 6 feet from the edge of a paved or usable shoulder, or 12 feet from the edge of the traveled way. *See* 2E–5. The OMUTCD gives exceptions to this general rule, such as when sidewalks physically impede this from being done. Still, it's something to look at.

What I've done here is provided you with some examples, and some of the more fruitful possibilities. But if you review the OMUTCD yourself regarding your specific case, you might, and probably will, find many other regulations that must be met to allow the executive branch, law enforcement, to enforce the traffic regulation against you.

When at trial, if you offer credible evidence establishing that the applicable traffic signs don't meet the OMUTCD standards, and the prosecution doesn't offer evidence to contradict or rebut yours, then this fact itself is an inconsistency that you must stress in your motion for a judgment of acquittal and your closing argument. *See* City of Mentor v. Mills, (11th District Court of Appeals, Lake County 1988).

A possible tactic

If you haven't filed any motions to dismiss based on failure to meet OMUTCD requirements, or filed any other motions letting the prosecution know you're going to conduct various measurements of the traffic signs in question, but you nonetheless offer the evidence as part of your case (say, for instance, you have a friend take the stand and introduce some photographs taken with him showing measurement of the traffic sign, or have him testify as to the height), then you have a very good chance of beating the case, in part because the prosecution *won't expect* you to do these measurements and present them at trial.

Since you didn't file any motions tipping him off, he won't be able to present any evidence countering or rebutting yours. This may be enough to win. You must weigh use of this tactic against a strong case that you may have (say the traffic sign is 4 feet high) that a motion to dismiss will be granted and save you the trouble and risk of trial.

Note: Introducing Pictures into evidence. If you want to introduce a picture into evidence, here's the basic way how. First, as with all your documents you'll introduce, have them marked as an exhibit number. The court will provide you stickers to do this, or you may use your own. Mark it exhibit 1 or 2, or whatever order you are introducing them in. Second, call your friend who is in the picture or was with you when you took the picture as a witness. Next, you might ask the following questions:

Q. Where were you on July 4th?

A. Well, I was with you.

Q. What were we doing?

A. We went to the place where you were pulled over and took some pictures of the signs and the road.

Q. Your honor, I have what is marked as exhibit 1. (Show the prosecutor the picture) May I approach the witness?

Judge: You may.

Q. I'm handing you what is marked as exhibit 1. (Hand him the picture) Do you recognize this?

A. Yes.

Q. What is it?

A. This is one of the pictures we took.

Q. How do you recognize it?

A. Well, I'm in the photograph. That's what I was wearing that day. That's the area we photographed. And I went with you to get the film developed. That was one of the pictures that were developed.

Q. What approximate time was the picture taken?

A. We were there from about 10 to 11 A.M., and took numerous pictures, so around that timeframe.

Q. Is this a fair and accurate depiction of the area as it was that day?

A. Yes.

Q. Is this picture in substantially the same condition as it was when you first saw it?

A. Yes.

Q. Thank you. (Take the picture from him. Walk back to where you were standing) Your honor, I offer exhibit 1 into evidence.

Judge (To the prosecutor): Any objections?

Prosecutor: Your honor, can I get a copy of his questions, he sure did a good job?

Traffic signals

The OMUTCD says, "Many laymen believe that traffic signals provide the solution to all traffic problems at intersections." *See* 6B–3. *Noooo*—that's what *law enforcement* believes. Laymen generally believe that a good *butt kicking* is the proper solution to most traffic problems *anywhere*. They go on to say, "This has led to their installation at a large number of locations where no legitimate factual warrant exists." Let us see why.

Traffic studies and warrants

There is a list of eleven so-called *warrants* in the OMUTCD for installation of traffic signals. Warrants are simply justifications for putting up a traffic signal. They are:

1. Minimum Vehicular Volume
2. Interruption of Continuous Traffic

3. Minimum Pedestrian Volume

4. School Crossings

5. Progressive Movement

6. Accident Experience

7. Systems

8. Combination of Warrants

9. Four Hour Volume

10. Peak Hour Delay

11. Peak Hour Volume

As the OMUTCD notes, generally traffic control signals shouldn't be installed unless one or more of these warrants is met. *See* 6C–2. These warrants represent the "minimum levels at which signal operation may be desirable." Furthermore, "[a] traffic study by a traffic engineer shall be the only basis for the installation of a signal unless at least one of the warrants specified in the Manual is met. The study shall identify the specific conditions which render the warrants inapplicable." *See* 6C–2.

Also, such a traffic study should include at the least a study of the various factors provided in each warrant, above. What does this all mean? It means you should be requesting the traffic study in discovery. *See* Appendix on Forms, Discovery Request. You should be motioning for their discovery if necessary. Or you should be motioning for their production at trial. *See* Appendix on Forms, Production. If they haven't done this traffic study, or if done, it isn't done properly (for instance, it doesn't identify the specific conditions which render the warrants inapplicable), then you have a strong case for dismissal. Again, talk with the county or township engineer, or the engineer with jurisdiction over that traffic area, to try and get this traffic study. Get this traffic study as soon as possible. Read over the warrants in the OMUTCD.

I'd bet my bottom dollar, considering Ticket-gate (read the preface), that there are scores of lights (both steady and flashing) out there that people are being ticketed on that aren't even official traffic signals.

Let's briefly discuss the first warrant, Minimum Vehicular Volume, to give an idea of them and show how they're *not* simplistic. They take some work that it's not clear every local authority is willing to do. Warrant 1 has to do with controlling a substantial amount of traffic through the intersection of a major street and a high volume minor street. This warrant is satisfied when for every hour of any 8 hours of an average day, one of the following occurs:

1. If the major and minor streets are one lane, then if there are 500 vehicles per hour (vph) on the major street and 150vph on the minor street.

2. If the major street is two or more lanes and the minor street is one lane, then if there is 600vph on the major street and 150vph on the minor street.

3. If the major and minor streets are two or more lanes, then if there is 600vph on the major street and 200vph on the minor street.

4. If the major street is one lane and the minor street is two or more lanes, then if there is 500vph on the major street and 200vph on the minor street.

The major and minor street volumes must be calculated for the same 8 hours. If the community is smaller, then smaller figures apply (I won't go into them; I don't want to get you too excited about all this). That's just Warrant 1. Still think they're doing the traffic studies?

Size and design

Only two sizes are allowed: 8 or 12 inches in diameter. An 8-inch red indication can never be used in combination with a 12-inch circular green or yellow indication. *See* 6B–8. If the approach to an intersection has both traffic control and lane-use control signals operating simultaneously for a driver, the 12-inch diameter must be used. Thus, if it's an intersection that twists, requiring use of lane-use control (such as arrows) to direct you, then the light above better be 12 inches in diameter. Otherwise, your ticket will be voided. Remember, you can motion to dismiss. There are other times when a 12-inch diameter signal is required. Check the OMUTCD for them.

Height

If your dealing with a traffic light mounted over a roadway, it's height above the pavement grade at the center of the roadway must be between 15 and 19 feet. If it's 14 feet, it's no good. If it's 20 feet, it's no good. If it's the type not mounted over a roadway, it must be between 8 and 15 feet. *See* 6B–13.

There you are. This should give you plenty of ammo to fight any traffic sign or signal ticket. They're out there…those unofficial signs. Be sure to look over the OMUTCD yourself. It's packed full of good information. The OMUTCD stated, "All unofficial signs should be removed, as they weaken the value of traffic signs." *See* 2A–3. When you realize how many traffic control devices out there are unofficial, and yet are still being enforced against fellow citizens, it should weaken more than the value of the traffic signs and it should strengthen your resolve to challenge them.

11

RADAR and LASER

Before getting into what's generally required of a radar device in order to convict you of a speed violation based on it, let me say a few words about radar detectors.

It pays to get a radar detector.

First off, they work. They work well. Don't let the critics and authorities fool you. There are ticket defense books that say radar detectors don't work well against hand held radars, because the radar is only on when the police officer pushes the button. One word: Bull. Once the officer pushes that button, your radar detector will sound off. Then you steadily slow down. There are other things besides shooting your car with electromagnetic radiation for two seconds that the police officer must do in order to secure a speeding violation. *See* below (example: tracking history). There's an old wives tale out there that if a police officer sees you applying your breaks in this type of situation, they'll ticket you for sure. One word: Double Bull. What law are they going to ticket you under, the one that doesn't allow you to legally apply your brakes?! Show me it; I want to see it. Other ticket defense books report the 'general belief ' that if you do have a radar detector, when an officer pulls you over she's more likely to cite you. One word: Triple Bull. What in the heck is she pulling you over for in the first place? She won't have a reason to. Your radar detector *detected* her radar, you slowed down, she doesn't have any idea you were speeding, end of story. What's she going to do, pull you over and give you a ticket for having a legal radar detector?! The way some of these traffic ticket defense books talk, you'd think *they* were in on the ticket scam. Having a radar detector may in fact deter shifty police officers from issuing bogus tickets.

Radar detectors are legal in Ohio and the vast majority of states, as long as you're not a rigger (trucker).

Radar detectors are inexpensive. You can get an excellent radar detector for around $50–100 at various stores, sometimes less if on sale. Call around. Make sure and get one with cloaking capability—a 'radar detector-detector protector.' Some police forces have devices that tell them you have a radar detector on board by detecting the electromagnetic signature your radar detector puts out. These are called radar detector-detectors. Well, technology will never be outdone. Modern radar detectors detect such a device. Hence the name radar detector-detector protector, or simply cloaking device.

Lastly, these radar detectors also effectively detect lasers, though you'll have a smaller amount of reaction time. With lasers though, once your detector detects it and you use the appropriate evasive measures (which *doesn't* mean braking and swerving like a madman; that'll just produce a separate ticket), the police officer, especially an inexperienced one, will have a difficult time keeping the laser pinpointed on your vehicle, resulting in poor aiming or panning on and off the target (laser targets are particular *parts* of your vehicle; those which are sufficiently reflective, such as your license plate). This generates sweep error.

Basically, the laser never effectively acquires the target, and may give an error message. Indeed, it's come to a highway version of high-tech information warfare. With the advent of every new technological mode of tyranny, an opposing technological mode of autonomy is assured.

Nowadays law enforcement, including the prosecutor's office, has a fairly tight grip on radar-based speeding tickets. They've seen all kinds of defenses, and so have *institutionally* (not necessarily *individual* prosecutors, some of which are beyond hope) matured to deal with them. I won't kid you here. I'm not saying you don't have a chance. What this means is that your probability of success will be highly dependent on the judge's temperament and the prosecutor's experience or, if they're not experienced, then on their motivation and training.

Frequently, juvenile traffic ticket prosecutors are less experienced than adult traffic ticket prosecutors. But you never know.

Here are the basic radar/laser elements the prosecutor must show (*See*, for instance, City of East Cleveland v. Ferell, 154 N.E.2d 630: read as volume 154, book N.E.2d, page 630: ask your local law librarian for assistance):

1 The *general type* of radar/laser used is accurate and reliable.
   a. This can be done by what's called judicial notice, *or*
   b. Testimony as to the general type of radar.
2 The *particular unit* used for the citation was in good operating condition at the time.
   a. That the officer was *qualified to test and calibrate* the unit.
      i. Introducing a certificate of training and/or the officer's testimony can show this.
   b. That the officer *properly tested and calibrated* the unit on the day of the citation, before the citation.
      i. Introducing certificates of accuracy/testing and/or the officer's testimony can show this.
      ii. Radar tests covered should include an internal calibration test for testing and calibrating the internal circuitry, and an external calibration test (using tuning forks) to test the radars recognition of external sources. Both tests should be done in the radar's stationary *and* moving

modes. The tests should be done before *and* after the officer's shift.

iii. Laser tests covered should include a scope alignment test to ensure the laser is aiming and aligned properly, and a calibration test to assure the laser is measuring speed and distance properly. These tests should be done before *and* after the officer's shift.

iv. All of these tests should be logged in the officer's calibration log, which you can get access to requesting it during discovery or by requesting production of the logbook for trial.

3 The officer using the particular unit was *qualified to use* the unit.

a. Introducing a certificate of training and/or the officer's testimony can show this.

4 The officer using the particular unit *properly used* the unit.

a. The *officer visually identified* your vehicle as speeding and continued tracking this identification throughout. This is a crucial factor in the officer's 'tracking history' of your vehicle, which typically continues until your vehicle has passed out of the radar beam, or until your vehicle has passed the officer's vehicle, *and*

b. The *radars visual* display indicated a violation, *and*

c. The *radars audio* monitor indicated that the officer's visually identified vehicle and the radars visual display identify the same vehicle. The audio output is also part of the officer's tracking history.

That's the gist of it. You see there is considerable potential for error or carelessness, for the police officer and the prosecutor. This means there's potential for producing inconsistencies. What you have to do is look at these various elements in light of your particular case circumstances, and see where a weakness might be. You also have to pay attention at trial, to ensure the prosecutor goes over each section suf-ficiently. *See* Producing Inconsistencies, Radar.

Here's a little technical stuff, in case you're interested, on how the pros-ecutor will try and introduce the various certificates into evidence.

Introducing certificates

At trial, the prosecution will probably try and introduce into evidence a certificate of accuracy (among other certificates) for the radar/laser detector used to ticket you. They will do this through the police officer that ticketed you. Assume the prosecutor has the *original* certificate. The prosecutor will say something like, "Your honor, I have what is marked as exhibit 1 (shows you the certificate). May I approach the wit-ness?" Judge, "You may."

Q. Officer, I'm handing you what has been marked as exhibit 1. Do you recognize this?

A. Yes.

Q. What is it?

A. This is the certificate of accuracy for the radar device I used that day.

Q. How do you know that?

A. Well, it's got the date on it right here. And I just remember.

Q. Whose signature is on it?

A. Mine and the Captain's. We signed it when we tested it.

Q. When was that?

A. Before I went out on the road that day.

The prosecutor may ask a number of questions about the officer's test-ing of the radar.

The prosecutor will then say, "Your honor, the state offers exhibit 1 into evidence." He might also wait and ask this later. But he *must* ask it before he rests his case, or the certificate is not in evidence, and you can motion for acquittal based on insufficient evidence. The judge may not grant the motion, since introduction of the certificate isn't necessarily required to establish accuracy. The officer's testimony may be sufficient. But it's certainly worth the try.

If you're interested in this kind of stuff, here's one way to try and throw the prosecutor, who, you'll remember, is perhaps a green legal intern, a curveball. Assume, as is often the case, that it *isn't the original* certificate of accuracy. The police officer just brought in a copy. You'll know because before the prosecutor shows the police officer the certificate, or does anything with it, he has to let you look at it. If he doesn't, just stand up and politely ask the judge if you can look at it. The prosecutor goes through the line of questioning above, and asks, "Your honor, the state offers exhibit 1 into evidence." Now you can object, stand and say, "Objection, your honor. On two grounds. First, the Best Evidence Rule. Your honor, considering the importance of this document to the case, the original should be required unless a copy is properly authenticated. There is question as to the authenticity of the Captain's signature." Authenticity means that something is what it claims to be. How does anyone really know it's the Captain's signature if the Captain isn't there to testify, or if the prosecution doesn't establish it some other way? You continue, "Second, the certificate is not self-authenticating because there's no evidence that it was properly certified." That'll throw everyone for a loop. Even if you don't win on the objection, it'll be amusing watching the expressions on their faces; prosecutor's, when dealing with *pro se* defendants (defendants who don't use a lawyer), typically think that they, and they only, have access to this esoteric legalese. The legal intern may not even know what you're talking about, and will rely on the judge to save him. The judge may or may not save him. Indeed, if the judge likes your argument, she may ask the prosecutor for a response to your objection. If he *is* befuddled, you may have just won your case.

12

VASCAR and Pennsylvania aerial, stopwatches and RADAR

The acronym VASCAR sounds ominously high-tech. It's not. It's basically a stopwatch hooked up to a calculator. VASCAR stands for Visual Average Speed Computer And Recorder. Impressive. The government must show that the VASCAR was properly tested and used over an accurate distance. Producing inconsistencies in VASCAR will generally come from the officer's *use* of it, or from evidence showing an inaccurate distance that it was used over. *See* Producing Inconsistencies Section, VASCAR.

As for stopwatches, in Ohio the prosecution must show the ground distance was measured, and measured accurately, that the stopwatch was accurate and that it was properly used. Stopwatch inconsistencies generally come from officer use, much as with the VASCAR. Although it happens that the prosecution may forget to have the officer testify as to the accuracy of the distance: how it was measured, and so if it was in fact measured accurately. Case dismissed.

Pennsylvania electronic stopwatches and radar

Did you know that Pennsylvania law enforcement recently set a new year-record for the number of speeding tickets issued on the PA Turnpike? Did you also know that Pennsylvania is ranked number two among states for the total number of speeding tickets issued? Number one?—Ohio.[10]

PA stopwatches are a separate animal. PA electronic stopwatches are used for PA turnpike aerial observation speeding tickets, and are governed by numerous regulations. Since I will cover this PA traffic phenomenon in the Producing Inconsistencies section, PA stopwatch regulations require mentioning. *These procedures also apply to the use of radar*, and they *don't just apply to turnpike speeding tickets*, but to speeding tickets in general across the Commonwealth of Pennsylvania. Though the rules are generally applicable, I focus on PA turnpike aerial observation tickets because I have particular experience in this area.

You might wonder how. Well, I am the proud owner of a laser-red 2001 Ford Mustang GT. I'm also the proud owner of a great radar detector that, of course, doesn't detect stopwatches. My brother lives near Pittsburgh. We frequently golf together. I frequently drive the PA turnpike to meet up with him, golf bags in trunk, golf shoes on and all. Enough said?

Throughout, I will be citing to Pennsylvania statutes and cases. The law librarian at your local law library can help you with the case citations, but it's fairly simple. Example: 539 A.2d 814: 539 is the volume, A.2d is the book, 814 is the page number. Just go to the law library, ask where the 'A 2d.' books are (show them the case citation), and look the case up.

Here are three things the PA prosecutor must show beyond a reasonable doubt. *See* Commonwealth v. Kittelberger, 616 A.2d 1:

1 They must show that the general type of stopwatch at issue was a *PA Department of Transportation (DOT) authorized device.*

   a. The court may take judicial notice of this element if the prosecution shows DOT approval in the Pennsylvania Bulletin. See Commonwealth v. Kittelberger, 616 A.2d 1.

2 They must show that the stopwatch was tested at a *DOT appointed testing* station.

   a. The certificate of accuracy cannot be used to show this. It must be shown by independent evidence. *See* Commonwealth v. Denny, 539 A.2d 814; Commonwealth v. Perdok, 192 A.2d 221.

   b. An employee of the testing station cannot attest to the fact that it is a DOT appointed testing station. *See* Commonwealth v. Denny.

   c. The court may take judicial notice of this element if prosecution shows DOT approval in the Pennsylvania Bulletin. *See* Commonwealth v. Denny.

3 They must introduce into evidence the stopwatch's *certificate of accuracy* issued by the DOT approved testing station.

   a. The certificate must show on its face (in writing) that the stopwatch was tested within 60 days of your citation. *See* Commonwealth v. Gernsheimer, 419 A.2d 528. Note this case also stands for the proposition that the certificate "must be signed by the person conducting the tests *and* the engineer in charge of the testing station" (italics added)...a fact you may want to keep in mind. When the prosecutor shows you the certificate, and it only has the officer's signature, doesn't have the engineer's signature, or no testimony was offered verifying that it was signed by the engineer, you may try to motion for acquittal at the appropriate time and cite this case to the judge.

b. This certificate *cannot* be introduced into evidence unless they have *first* shown that it was a DOT appointed testing station that tested and issued the certificate. (Objection: lack of foundation). *See* Commonwealth v. Denny.

c. If it isn't the *original* certificate, then the *photocopy must* be authenticated (shown that it is a fair and accurate copy of the original). *See* Commonwealth v. Gordon, 633 A.2d 1199. If the officer at trial hasn't *seen* the original (which may occur if he wasn't the one who tested and signed the certificate), then he can't testify to the copy being an accurate representation of the original (Objection: personal knowledge and qualification to authenticate). If he has seen the original, and doesn't testify to authentication, then the certificate is inadmissible. (Objection: lack of foundation). *If* the prosecution claims that the copy is 'self-authenticating,' then it must have been certified by the custodian or other person authorized to certify. This certification must bear a seal purporting to be that of Pennsylvania, or a political subdivision or agency thereof, and the custodian's signature attesting to the authenticity of the copy. (Objection: Lack of proper certification to self-authenticate). *If* there is no seal, then a separate public officer having official duties in Pennsylvania, and with a seal must have certified that the signature without the seal on the certificate of accuracy is genuine, and the signer has the official capacity to certify such documents. This person can only do this by separate certification with his own seal. **Wow! Lawyers *are* boneheads.** Truth is, it's for your own good. The documents that the government wants to use against you better not be fakes! That's the gist of this rigmarole. Not only that, but if the prosecutor doesn't know what he's doing, then this is a good way of excluding the certificate, thereby having your case dismissed. *See* Producing Inconsistencies Section, PA Aerial, for more. Also see the end of Chapter 11, Introducing Certificates, for more.

If you decide to make one of these objections to the certificate, you should make them when the prosecutor asks the judge to admit them into evidence. The prosecutor will ask the judge, "You honor, the state offers exhibit 1 into evidence." The judge should ask if you have any objections. Either way, if you have objections stand and say, "Your honor, I object to its admission on the following grounds…"

Statutes covering Pennsylvania speeding and stopwatches are: Title 75, Vehicles, §3368(d) (Speed timing devices); Title 67, DOT Vehicle Code, §105.71-75 (various: approved stopwatches, appointment of stopwatch testing station, etc.)

Don't forget that they must show they measured your speed over an *accurately measured* distance. If the officer doesn't testify to measuring the distance out with a tape measure, or odometer, or offering other official documentation verifying the distance they allege you were measured over was in fact that distance, then motion for a judgment of acquittal on these grounds.

There is further discussion on Pennsylvania turnpike tickets in the Producing Inconsistencies Section.

13

School buses, police cars and uniforms

School buses

There are some interesting regulations concerning school buses. First, the Department of Public Safety (DPS) must specially license any purported school bus driver. *See* §4511.763–TL. Also, a school bus cannot be operated unless it is registered with the superintendent of the state highway patrol and bears an identifying number assigned by the superintendent. *See* §4511.764–TL. School buses must be equipped with flashing red and amber lights. *See* §4511.771–TL. Also, the state highway patrol must inspect every school bus every year. A school bus cannot be operated unless it bears the inspection decal issued by the superintendent of the state highway patrol. *See* §4511.761–TL. How can you check for the existence or non-existence of such requirements? You can call the Department of Public Safety to check on the bus driver's license. You can contact the state highway patrol to check on the registration and inspection. You can also file a specific motion with the clerk of courts and the prosecutor requesting production of these documents at trial. *See* Appendix on Forms. Finally, you might try requesting them through the discovery process. *See* Chapter 5.

How can this help you? Well, if the documents don't exist, and the DPS gives you paperwork that shows the bus driver isn't licensed, it can be of immense help. For example, say you check and find out that the bus driver who ratted you out was in fact not specially licensed by the DPS to be a bus driver (The driver of the bus *wasn't* a bus driver: see how law turns logic on its head?). At pre-trial or trial during preliminary motions, you bring this issue up and request dismissal of your case, "Your honor, the bus driver was in fact not a bus driver at all (show the judge the paperwork from the DPS). He had no authority to be on the road. For this reason I request dismissal of my ticket." Technically this motion won't work; for one thing, there's no requirement of being a legal bus driver in order to report the violation. But you never know. The judge just might be in the mood to teach the prosecutor or the bus driver a lesson. Say it doesn't work. Then when you get the opportunity to cross-examine him you ask questions like:

Q. Sir, you claimed to see my vehicle on January 32nd?

A. Well, I didn't know it was your vehicle at the time.

Q. You only found out today?

A. Yes.

Q. You claim to have seen the license plate number: 31701?

A. Yes.

Q. You wrote it down soon after, I take it?

A. Like I told the prosecutor.

Q. You have special documents for reporting such things?

A. Yes.

Q. And you dutifully filled this one out?

A. Right.

Q. Because you're required to, right?

A. Uh-huh.

Q. You've been working as a bus driver for one and a half years now?

A. Right.

Q. And how many times have you filled out such paperwork?

A. About ten times.

Q. Each time you did, it was as a bus driver observing what you considered to be a violation?

A. Yep.

Q. Ever know what happened with these reports?

A. Uh, no I don't.

Q. Ever testify in court as to any of them?

A. One time.

Q. When?

A. Six months ago.

Q. And the person was convicted?

A. Yes, I believe so.

Q. And the other nine times, they probably pled guilty?

Objection: Speculation.

Response (you): He can answer if he doesn't know.

Judge: He can answer if he doesn't know.

A. Maybe. I don't know.

Q. Truth is though, sir, each time you dutifully filled these forms out against people you didn't do it as a bus driver, did you?

A. Yeah I did, I was driving the bus.

Q. But you were never licensed to drive the bus, were you?

A. Well, no, I guess not. (See below for if answer is yes)

Q. And when you testified in court against that person before, you weren't a licensed bus driver then either, were you sir?

A. No.

Q. Because you were never licensed by the department of public safety, were you?

A. No.

Q. Because you never dutifully applied for a license, did you?

A. Right.

Q. Even though you're required to do so; it's your duty to do so?

A. Yes, I guess so.

Q. You never dutifully filled out this required paperwork?

A. No.

Q. Though your boss told you to fill out this paperwork?

A. Right.

Q. And checked up on this and told you to do it on a number of occasions?

Et cetera. The basic point is this bus driver is a lazy chump…how can we trust what he says he saw? In case the answer to the question, "But you were never licensed to drive the bus, were you?" is "Yes," the following is applicable (remember, this questioning depends on you having done your homework and found out that he wasn't licensed):

Q. I suppose you have the paperwork from the department of public safety with you today showing you were licensed?

A. I'm supposed to be licensed with the department of public safety?

Q. Yes, it's required that you fill out paperwork. You didn't know that?

A. No.

Q. Your boss never told you that?

A. No.

Q. So you never filled out the paperwork?

A. No.

Q. And so you're not licensed?

A. I guess not.

Or—

Q. I suppose you have the paperwork from the department of public safety with you today showing you were licensed?

A. No, I don't.

Q. But you're saying that in fact you are licensed?

A. Yes.

Q. And if, say, I were to go and check with the department, I would find paperwork documenting such?

A. Yes.

Q. What would you think if paperwork was produced today showing you *weren't* licensed?

A. Well.

Now, the judge will either allow you to show the witness this paperwork, and then see what happens. It's objectionable, and depends on the formality of the hearing, or you may have to take the stand and testify as to receiving this document from the Department of Public Safety. Either way, the critical thing is for the judge to *see* this document and hear the witness testify as to his being licensed. The judge will be assessing his credibility all the while.

The main point of this cross-examination is to bring *equity* into play. Fairness—the great leveler. It's not so nice that this driver of a bus who's not a bus driver can go around filling out official reports that the state will rely on to prosecute people and convict them of *crimes*, when the driver himself, and the boss allowing him to drive, are not abiding by the law. That's the idea you want to bring out in your closing argument. When you've got a good legal backdrop in traffic court, equity can play a telling role. Inconsistency with *equity*, if communicated properly, is often more powerful than any *legal* breach.

Remember, you don't have to memorize your questions. You can type them up, write them down, and question from the paper if you like. Just be confident, professional and sincere. Also be incredulous at times, if it feels right for you. Getting the point across is the key.

Police cars and uniforms

There are two pertinent regulations concerning traffic officers. First, if a police officer is on duty for the main purpose of enforcing the traffic laws, they must wear a distinctive uniform. *See* §4549.15. This means the official uniform of whatever police department they're on. If they begin describing, "what happened that day," and they haven't testified to wearing the appropriate uniform, then object. The prosecutor, not having asked about the uniform requirements, asks, "Officer, tell us what happened that day." You stand and address the court, "Objection, your honor, lack of foundation. Your honor, the prosecution hasn't established that the officer is qualified to testify as to what happened that day." The judge might know what you're hinting at, and sustain (rule for you) the objection. On the other hand, the judge might think you're just making things up, and either ask you to clarify, or just over-rule (rule against you) your objection. If she overrules your objection, say, "Your honor, I request a continuing objection throughout the officer's testimony."

Second, if on duty for enforcing the traffic laws, the police motor vehicle used must be marked in some distinctive manner, and must be equipped with at least one flashing, oscillating, or rotating colored light mounted outside or on top of the vehicle. *See* §4511.13–TL. This means that the motor vehicle must bear the official markings and emblems of whatever police department they're on. The same question-objection scenario applies as with the officer's uniform.

Either way, what should happen if this *does* occur is that when the prosecutor rests: "The state rests your honor," it will be your turn. You now motion for a judgment of acquittal, as follows: "Your honor, I motion for acquittal based on an inadmissibility and insufficiency of evidence. In particular, the prosecution didn't establish a proper foundation qualifying the officer to testify. The officer didn't testify as to wearing an official police uniform (and/or) operating an official police vehicle on the day of the incident. That being the case, none of his testimony was properly admissible, and so the prosecution hasn't offered sufficient evidence to prove my guilt beyond a reasonable doubt."

Section Four

Producing Inconsistencies

14

To begin with

This section is dedicated to listing possible inconsistencies, and ways of producing inconsistencies, in the government's case against you. You should develop a checklist of your best avenues for producing inconsistencies, and focus on these areas first. This relies on proper application of sections II and III. I'll go into detail with some of the possibilities; I'll simply list other more obvious ones. Realize that this isn't an exhaustive list of possible inconsistencies or ways to produce inconsistencies. You'll probably think of or find other ways. God bless you.

15

Your ticket and witnesses

Your ticket and the law you were cited for violating are the groundwork. So first things first, analyze your ticket. You may save yourself a lot of trouble by discovering that the officer cited you under the wrong statute, or didn't write down a number at all.

Case in point—a driver is cited under §4511.43(A)–TL, which concerns the right-of-way at stop signs, when all the evidence shows the incident involved a yield sign, requiring citation under §4511.43(B).

Another good example: you may be incorrectly charged under one of the §4511.21–TL speeding provisions—where the you were cited under §4511.21(A), and then the ticket notes, for instance, 37mph in a 25mph. The ticket then further notes the good weather conditions, the light traffic, dry pavement, et cetera, and checks the 'Over limits' box while not checking the 'Unsafe for cond.' box. Well, this is nice and all, but if the driver knew what §4511.21(A) said, then she might be pretty happy. Since, as you know from referring back to it, §4511.21(A) covers (hold on, let me refer back to it)…driving at speeds greater or less than is *reasonable or proper*. It doesn't define any quantifiable 'limits,' like the 25mph the officer identified. The officer should have cited you under §4511.21(C). As a final example, you may be ticketed for a §4511.20–TL violation, when in fact it should have been a §4511.201–TL violation, or vice versa.

If you're incorrectly charged, or there's no statute number on the ticket (which amounts to the same thing as being incorrectly charged), tell the judge/magistrate at arraignment, and ask for your case to be dismissed. If it's already past the arraignment proceedings, then first speak with the prosecutor who is handling your case, and see if he'll dismiss the ticket. If not, then file a Motion to Dismiss as soon as possible with the clerk of courts and the prosecutor. If you're a juvenile and you've reached the pre-trial or trial stage, or you're an adult and you've reached the trial stage, the prosecutor may attempt to amend the ticket by asking the judge, "Your honor, the state motions to amend the ticket to change the section the defendant was cited under from §4511.43(A) to §4511.43(B)." The judge should ask you if you have any objections to this. Even if she doesn't, stand and say, "Objection, your honor. This amendment would change the name and identity of the crime I was charged with, and so is not permitted under Rule 7(D) of the Rules of Criminal Procedure."

If you've reached the pre-trial or trial stage, and the prosecutor *doesn't* ask to amend the ticket, then you should motion to the court, in your preliminary motions before trial begins, for a dismissal based on this incorrect citation. The judge, "Do you have any matters to cover or motions to make before trial begins?" You, "Yes, your honor. I motion to dismiss the case for a defect in the ticket. Your honor, the police officer cited me under §4511.43(A), but he should have cited me under §4511.43(B)." The judge, "Shouldn't you have raised this objection a while ago?" You, "Your honor, I would've raised this objection earlier, and before trial today, but I only realized the defect yesterday, while I was reading over the statute again to prepare for today. Your honor, this court may, in the interests of justice, allow this motion to be made today." She may tell you she's fully aware of what she can and cannot do, which is fine, or she may ask for further explanation, and you'll be on your way to a dismissal. Just make sure to always object to prosecutorial attempts to amend your ticket. Even if you don't know the exact reason, object anyhow and the judge might assist you.

Juveniles, remember the §2151.021 requirement discussed in Chapter 7. *Don't* motion to dismiss based on this requirement. *Only* use this requirement to motion for a judgment of acquittal. If you motion to dismiss on this ground, the court may allow amendment of the traffic ticket to include §2151.021 for procedural reasons.

As for witnesses, if you've received discovery from the prosecutor you'll have received, among other things, contact information for any and all witnesses they plan to call to the stand. If you're a juvenile, you should have also received any and all statements that witnesses have made. Think about what you're going to ask before you get in touch with the witnesses. Also look at the elements that the government must prove before you get in touch with them. You'll want to focus your questions on probing for weaknesses in any of the elements. Take notes. Try to discern if the witness *really saw* the incident, how well they remember what happened and how they explain what happened. This will give you an idea on how they'll testify, and if there are any conflicts in the facts. If there's more than one witness, say a police officer and another witness, then you might find that their stories conflict, which, if you can produce this at trial, is a good thing. Always be confident, courteous and professional. At all times. When in court, don't start arguing and saying things like, "Well, *you* told me when I talked to you two weeks ago that…" That's very objectionable. Plus, it won't get you anywhere; actually it will, it will probably get you convicted. The purpose of this witness questioning is to probe for weaknesses in the government's case, not to criticize the witness. Just remember, every witness is on your side…it's up to you to find out how.

It's the same with any and all other evidence, documents, photographs, et cetera. There's always an inconsistency in there somewhere. It doesn't have to be an utterly obvious, in-the prosecutor's-face admission of your non-guilt finding. Remember, the slightest inconsistency can create a reasonable doubt.

16

Producing inconsistencies in various cases

Even if you haven't been cited for this or that violation, I highly recommend that you read through, if nothing more that skimming, the different sections in this chapter. I often write about more than just the violation itself, considering topics such as cross-examination, taking the stand, getting documents, investigation and who knows what else. It will probably give you some good information and ideas. Also, an example of a direct examination is in the right-of-way section. Nevertheless, still go to your applicable section first.

Speeding

Regardless if you're caught with radar, laser, vascar, aircraft, or what have you, even if you *were* traveling faster than the officially posted legal speed limit if you can show that your driving was *reasonable under the circumstances* you *must* be found not guilty. *See,* for example, State v. Nedelkoff, 263 N.E. 2d 803; Kirtland Hills v. McGrath, 624 N.E.2d 255 (46mph in an urban district); State v. Bratten, 236 N.E.2d 683 (80mph in a 70mph zone). (To read these cases, understand that, for instance with 263 N.E.2d 803: 263 is the volume, N.E.2d is the book, 803 is the page number. Go to your local law library and ask the law librarian where their N.E. 2d books are (show them the citation), and find the case.)

This is a great defense if you've got the right information on your side, which you frequently will. This defense is only applicable in states, like Ohio, where the speed limits are prima facie. To find out if it applies in your state, look at the applicable speeding laws, and see if they have provisions like Ohio's. If so, you're good to go. Also note there are a few speeding violations where this defense is inapplicable, such as speeding over a bridge, which is an 'absolute' speed limit.

What does reasonable under the circumstances mean? In determining if your driving was reasonable under the circumstances, the judge or jury can consider such factors as the weather (sunny, dry, windy, foggy, visibility, et cetera), the road (dryness, width, surface, straightaway or turn), traffic conditions (light, moderate, heavy), permanent physical features at the scene, time of day, and any other pertinent prevailing conditions existing at the time. No, the condition of *your* car doesn't count (old jalopies aren't allowed to drive unreasonably either)—"Your honor, if I would've slowed down, the front bumper would've fallen off!"

How do you find these things out? Look on your ticket, crazy! See the boxes marked Pavement, Visibility, Weather, Traffic, Area, Crash, and Remarks? Well, there you go. Also quite important, look at the box marked 'Unsafe for cond.', in the Speed section of your ticket. Besides this, which is extremely persuasive information, if you had a passenger then you've got a potential witness to the conditions.

First, some courts, if the officer didn't mark the 'Unsafe for cond.' box or didn't specifically include the statute number 4511.21(A) along with their speeding number (often 4511.21(C)), will dismiss your ticket. Just inform the judge at arraignment that your ticket wasn't filled out completely, that it's missing one or both of these entries, and so should be dismissed. Likewise, if after the arraignment, mention it at your pre-trial or preliminary motions before trial, or motion for dismissal on these grounds. *See* Appendix on Forms, Motion to Dismiss. It could be an easy way out of your ticket.

If you think about it, it makes sense. Since if the officer didn't mark the 'Unsafe for cond.' box, then you must have been driving in a manner safe for the conditions (cond.), and so reasonably under the circumstances. And if the officer didn't write 4511.21(A) down on your ticket, which covers driving "at a speed greater or less than is reasonable or proper, having due regard to the traffic, surface, and width of the street or highway and any other conditions," then a proper conclusion is that you *were* driving reasonably under the prevailing conditions. Remember, if the prosecutor tries to amend the ticket to include §4511.21(A), object, "Your honor, I object. This amendment would change the identity and name of the crime charged against me." You can also motion to dismiss based on these grounds, "Your honor, I motion to dismiss this ticket. It is not filled out completely. The unsafe for conditions box is not marked, and so the necessary inference is that I was driving safely under the conditions and so reasonably under the circumstances. Likewise, your honor, the officer didn't include section 4511.21(A) on my ticket, which implies that I was driving reasonably under the circumstances. Since I was driving reasonably under the circumstances, I have not violated the speed-limit provisions of section 4511.21." It's always a good idea to bring those case citations, or others you find on the subject, to court with you, in case the judge asks for them. Even better if you can get a copy of the case (or the pertinent sections) and highlight the applicable portions, then after you give your motion give the judge the applicable case law. She'll think you're all right.

Let's say the judge is in the mood to hear a trial that afternoon, and so denies your motion based on the above. The officer takes the stand, and after the prosecutor is done asking his questions, it's your turn to cross-examine the officer. You stand and ask,

Q. Sir, you cited me for going 37mph in a 25mph zone, correct?

A. That's correct.

Q. You just described the road to the prosecutor. You said the road was a straightaway?

A. The portion you were speeding on, yes.

Q. And you were located facing the direction I was approaching from?

A. Yes.

Q. Now, it was 1:42 in the afternoon? (The time should be on your ticket)

A. I think so.

Q. If that's the time written down on the ticket you gave me, then you'd agree?

A. Sure, of course.

Q. And you say you first saw me when I was about a quarter of a mile away? (He testified to this on direct exam with the prosecutor)

A. About 1000 feet away or so.

Q. And 1280 feet is a quarter of a mile?

A. Okay, sure.

Q. So it's fair to say you had good visibility of me?

A. Yes. (If he says no, then he's got a problem with his tracking history. See radar section, below)

Q. Now, the traffic conditions were moderate? (On your ticket)

A. Yes.

Q. Meaning there were a few cars dispersed on the road?

A. Pretty much, cars driving back and forth on various portions of the roadway.

Q. And it was sunny out?

A. Yeah, I think. Maybe it was partly cloudy.

Q. Well, there were no adverse weather conditions, were there?

A. If that's what I have on my ticket.

Q. It is. No rain?

A. No, it's probably written on my ticket.

Q. Indeed it is. No fog?

A. No, not that I can remember.

Q. Good weather, then?

A. Yes.

Q. And the road, it's a four lane road?

A. Yes, the part you were driving on.

Q. It's a well built road?

A. Sure, I guess.

Q. The pavement that time of day, it wasn't wet was it?

A. No.

Q. Wasn't snowy or icy?

A. No, it's on the ticket.

Q. Yes it is, sir. Also on the ticket is that there was no crash?

A. Right.

Q. In fact, a crash wasn't even *almost caused*, isn't that true? (On the ticket)

A. I don't believe so.

Q. Your honor, I have the ticket the officer has been referring to here. (Show the prosecutor the ticket) May I approach the witness, your honor?

Judge: You may.

Q. (Showing the officer the part of the ticket with the boxes Crash and 'Almost Caused' on it) I'm showing you the ticket we've been talking about. See here, the box 'Crash,' it's not marked is it?

A. No.

Q. And the box marked 'Almost Caused' isn't marked either, is it?

A. No, it isn't.

Q. (Walk back to your previous position, keeping the ticket) Sir, you may have also seen there were no remarks in the 'Remarks' section?

A. Right.

Q. And you didn't mark the unsafe for conditions box either?

A. I don't believe so.

Q. Your honor, may I approach the witness?

Judge: What for?

You: I would just like to show him the unsafe for conditions box, so the record can be clear whether he marked it or not.

Judge: All right.

Q. (Showing the officer the box) Here, the unsafe for conditions box isn't marked, is it?

A. No, it isn't.

Q. See also, you didn't write the statute number 4511.21(A) down, did you?

A. (Looks at ticket) No I didn't.

Q. (Walk back to your previous position, keeping the ticket) You only wrote down 4511.21(C)?

A. That's the section you violated.

Q. Not section 4511.21(A)?

A. No.

Q. You're familiar with section 4511.21(A), correct?

A. Yes. (If not, have a copy there to show him)

Q. And so you know that its provisions cover such things as, for instance, driving at reasonable speeds under the prevailing conditions?

A. Right, among other things.

Q. But you didn't cite me under section 4511.21(A)?

A. No.

Q. Because, as you said, the section I violated was 4511.21(C), and not 4511.21(A)?

A. Right, you violated 4511.21(C).

Q. Because I was driving reasonably under the prevailing conditions?

Objection: Asking for conclusion.

Response (you): Your honor, this is based on the officer's expertise, training and what he witnessed that day.

Judge: Sustained (rules against you)

Q. I was driving safely for the conditions?

Objection: Asking for conclusion.

Response: Your honor, the officer didn't mark the unsafe for conditions box. He can answer the question based on his training, experience, and what he witnessed that day.

Judge: Overruled (rules for you)

A. Could you repeat the question?

Q. I was driving safely for the conditions?

A. Well, you weren't driving *unsafely* for the conditions. You were speeding.

Q. *Not unsafely* you say?

If he's foolish enough to testify that he thinks you were driving unsafely for the conditions, or he says you were driving unreasonably (either on direct examination or during your cross-examination), then simply ask, "Well then, you didn't mark it on the ticket, did you sir?" Or, "Well then, you didn't cite me under 4511.21(A), which covers driving unreasonably, did you sir?" If he tries to explain *why* he didn't mark it that way then after he's done rambling, simply ask, "Sir, I didn't ask you *why* you didn't mark it. I simply asked if you marked it or not. And you didn't, did you sir?"

Remember, always be courteous, never be argumentative, *and always* be professional, sincere and confident. At the same time, have a bit of incredulity when appropriate.

You've beaten the horse as best you can. Understand, it's okay to separate out your questions like this, and ask what seems 'the obvious.' You're developing the record. You're emphasizing the conclusion you want made—that you were driving reasonably under the circumstances. You're being thorough.

Besides, *they* wanted the trial, not you. You were completely content to have the ticket dismissed. So give them a trial! Now, in your closing, you'll address all these points, one after the other, and argue that you were driving reasonably under the circumstances, and so not guilty. If you can, bring those cases, or others you find, to court, cite them during closing argument for the position you're arguing.

Lastly, keep in mind that there may be other types of inconsistencies in the ticket that you should tailor your cross-examination to. For instance, the ticket might mark unsafe for conditions, yet all the conditions marked for weather, traffic, crash, et cetera, might be marked inconsistently with this. By the way, on cross-examination don't ever ask the witness, "Why…?" You'll just give him a platform to justify any inconsistencies you've created.

Assured clear distance

You'll recall that assured clear distance tickets fall under §4511.21(A)–TL. There's substantial argument out there whether or not the mere occurrence of an accident, without other evidence, is enough to convict you of the charge. In legalese, the question is: is the accident prima facie evidence of a violation. Here we use prima facie to mean sufficient evidence to allow a reasonable juror to decide beyond a reasonable doubt that you did what you were charged with. There's an Ohio case that says the mere fact of a collision *doesn't* establish this violation. *See* Miller v. City of Dayton, 41 N.E.2d 728. That is, an accident isn't prima facie evidence of an assured clear distance charge.

This is the position you want to take. This means the prosecution *must produce more evidence*, i.e. a witness, to testify that you were driving too fast to permit you to bring it to a stop within the assured clear distance ahead. If they don't produce any witness at trial besides the officer testifying that she gave you a ticket (assuming she didn't witness the accident herself), when the prosecution is done their case, "The state rests," it's your turn. You motion for a judgment of acquittal, "Your honor, I motion for an acquittal based on an insufficiency in evidence. The prosecution didn't provide any evidence other that the police officer's testimony that there was an accident. But this alone isn't sufficient to prove I was driving at a speed that didn't permit me to stop within the assured clear distance. I have a case that stands for this proposition (Show him the case cited above, or at least cite the case)."

Also, assured clear distance charges only apply if the object is in front of you and, if moving, if moving in the same direction as you. It doesn't apply if, say, the car you collided with was coming from the opposite direction.

If they do bring another witness in, you'll want to cross-examine her, because the decision whether you violated the charge or not will depend on her testimony. First though, you want to clarify for the record that the officer didn't witness the accident.

> Q. Ma'am, just to clarify for the record, you weren't present when the accident occurred?
>
> A. No.
>
> Q. You arrived on the scene afterwards?
>
> A. Right.

Now you can ask the officer anything else you want, if you've discovered another inconsistency. Otherwise, your focus will be on the witness. You want to question the witness on her *observation/perception* of the accident. Also, there may be issues of the object that you hit (say a lifted manhole; I don't know, you think of one) not being *reasonably discernible*, or possibly the object you hit suddenly cut in to your path or quickly slowed down so that you couldn't avoid the collision. It will all depend on your case's particular circumstances.

Say the witness is the driver of the car in front of you, whose car you happened to hit in the rear bumper. Now, your cross-examination of her will be highly dependent on the information you got when you questioned her before trial. Remember, you requested and/or motioned for discovery, got her whereabouts and talked with her...right? Maybe she was in a rush to pick up her child from school, late for an appointment or what have you. Also, again, before you begin cross-examining her (adults) ask the judge to see any past statement she's made. Juveniles, you should have already received these through the discovery process. In this way, you'll be able to see where to focus your questions. If this is the star witness, and *she really didn't witness anything*, then it's weak evidence, and you've produced a clear inconsistency that you can hammer on in closing argument.

Furthermore, it's not enough that she witnessed the accident; if it were, then the police officer's testimony that there was an accident would be sufficient. *She has to witness enough circumstances* to establish beyond a reasonable doubt that you were driving too fast to permit your car from stopping within the assured clear distance, a highly fact-sensitive inquiry.

Q. Ma'am, the incident occurred at 2:55?

A. Yes.

Q. You were on your way to a doctor's appointment?

A. Right.

Q. At the local clinic?

A. Right.

Q. And that's about 5 miles away from where the accident occurred?

A. About that.

Q. Now, your appointment was for 3:00, right?

A. Yes, that's right.

Q. So you only had five minutes to get there on time?

A. Uh, yeah. (So her attention is on something else just before the accident occurred)

Q. You consider yourself a good driver?

A. Yes, I do.

Q. You pay attention to the cars around you?

A. Yes.

Q. You say you noticed my car behind you?

A. I noticed a car behind me.

Q. Because you glanced in your rear view mirror, like we all do?

A. Yes.

Q. You must have noticed a car in front of you too?

A. Of course.

Q. Because you were focused on driving?

A. Right.

Q. After you noticed my car?

A. Well, I'm not sure. Probably saw it before and after.

Q. So you glanced at my car in your rear view mirror, then looked and saw a car in front of you, then glanced at my car in your rear view mirror again?

A. Yes.

Q. And this occurred, you'd say five times? (What she testified to on direct exam) (Establishing that there was 'substantial' time in between sightings: the charge is that you were driving too fast to permit yourself to stop within the assured clear distance; if there are substantial time frames in between the collision and her sightings, then the argument is you weren't driving too fast to permit stopping)

A. About that. I was looking, watching…Aware of my surroundings. (Yeah, right, aren't we all)

Q. Then after a few moments, say five seconds, you heard a crash?

A. Yeah, about that, and felt it. You hit my car.

Q. And then you looked in your rear view mirror again to see what happened?

A. Yes.

Q. And you saw my car?

A. Yes, attached to my bumper.

Q. And you were watching the car in front of you in that five seconds or so between seeing my car and the collision?

A. Yes.

Q. Because you were watching where you were driving?

A. Of course.

Q. And then our cars collided?

A. Yes.

Q. So it's fair to say you didn't see the collision, right?

A. Uh-huh.

Q. And you glanced at my car, say, five times?

A. Yeah.

Q. And each time after seeing my car, you then looked ahead to watch where you were driving?

A. Yes.

In closing argument, you'll argue that she only glanced at your vehicle for a few, at most five, fleeting moments. Each time afterwards she had looked ahead to where she was driving. Her attention was on getting to her appointment. Her attention was concentrated mostly on the car in front of her. This, you'll argue, isn't solid enough evidence to prove the charge beyond a reasonable doubt. Yes, there was an accident, but that fact alone isn't enough to establish the crime.

The questions you ask for this type of charge will be highly dependent on the circumstances and what you find out before trial. Who is the witness? Was she in a hurry? How many times did she see your car, and for how long each time? What prior statements did she make? Does she have an eye prescription, and if so was she wearing her glasses that day? "Ma'am, I note you're wearing glasses today. You weren't wearing glasses the day of the incident, were you?" Did *she* brake abruptly? Any passengers in her car, like kids, that she has to pay heed to? If an adult passenger, were they having a discussion? What did they talk about? Anything to show her attention was somewhere else other than your car and the speed it was traveling. Remember, go into detail, be methodical, break your questions down, and always be sincere, polite, confident and professional.

Right-of-way

I reprint here the discussion of the concept of right-of-way from another portion of my book for your aid and enjoyment. This applies to flashing red stop signals, stop signs, and yield signs.

Right-of-way also applies when turning left at intersections and generally at intersections. Note it *doesn't* apply to flashing yellow caution signals, the law of which only stipulates that you may proceed. through such intersection "only with caution." *See* §4511.15(B)–TL (that's a different standard than all this other stuff).

Right-of-way means: The right of a vehicle, streetcar, trackless trolley, or pedestrian to proceed uninterruptedly in a *lawful* manner in the direction in which it or the individual is moving in preference to another vehicle, streetcar, trackless trolley, or pedestrian approaching from a different direction into its or the individual's path. *See* §4511.01(UU)(1)–TL.

Failure to yield

In the statutes, the right-of-way of a driver is *presumed* (the prosecutor doesn't have to prove it). For example, for §4511.41–TL, the prosecutor only has to show that your vehicle was indeed "on the left," or that the other vehicle was on the right. Once they've done this, the right-of-way of the other vehicle is presumed, and you'll have to offer evidence to show otherwise (for instance, that he was driving unreasonably and so forfeited the right-of-way). Nonetheless, the government must still prove *failure to yield* this right-of-way. Some people argue about what is necessary to establish the failure to yield element. Some say, absent evidence to the contrary, if there is an accident and the other driver had the right-of-way, the accident itself will be sufficient to establish that you failed to yield this right-of-way. Others say hogwash. They have to prove more than merely that an accident *occurred*. What do I say? Hell, argue every point you can and let the judge sort it out.

For instance, if you're interested in arguing this type of point, let's take §4511.43(B)–TL, concerning the right-of-way at yield signs. Go back and read the last sentence of §4511.43(B). It reads:

> Whenever a driver is involved in a collision with a vehicle or trackless trolley in the intersection or junction of roadways, after driving past a yield sign without stopping, the collision shall be prima facie evidence of the driver's failure to yield the right-of-way.

This means that if you went through a yield sign *without stopping*, and were involved in a collision, the collision will be prima facie evidence (used in this sense, the term means enough evidence in and of itself to allow a reasonable juror to decide beyond a reasonable doubt that you committed the element) of failure to yield.

This means all the prosecution will have to prove in evidence for the *failure to yield* element is that you were involved in a collision. Now, that's a luxury! But, to get this advantage, they'll have to prove, beyond a reasonable doubt, that you went through the yield sign *without stopping*. Once again, we're back to witnesses, their credibility (believability), their perception, and their prior statements.

This, as with any part, will be shot to the moon if you previously admitted the element to the police officer. Say you told the officer that you didn't stop at the yield sign. Well, then forget about fighting it. *No, you can't say the officer didn't read you your Miranda rights before you told him this, and so it's not admissible. Well, you can *say* it, but it won't work...for a number of reasons. One being that you volunteered the statement. Another being you weren't in custody. Now, don't get me wrong, you may have particular circumstances where your Miranda rights were infringed. If you have *any* doubt or question as to this, get a lawyer-consultation on it.

Back to the point, the statute specifically reads, "without stopping." So the question is just begging itself to be asked. What happens if you *did* stop, or correctly put, if there is a reasonable doubt as to the prosecution's case that you *didn't* stop (You don't have to prove you stopped, they have to prove you didn't)? Say they can't prove you didn't stop. Then, this last sentence of the law doesn't apply to your case. It only applies if you went through *without stopping*, which they can't prove. This means that they'll have to come up with evidence *above and beyond* the mere accident itself to prove you failed to yield the right-of-way.

What will that evidence be? Well, a witness of course. Back to perception, believability, bias, prior statements, et cetera. The witness is usually the other driver. Consider your cross-examination of him.

Q. Sir, my car was stopped, wasn't it?

A. I'm not sure; I didn't see it.

Q. You don't know if my car was stopped or not?

A. No, I couldn't say. All I know is I was driving down the road and you pulled out and I ran into you.

Note, you have already established a reasonable doubt with the last answer.

Q. But you didn't see my car until after I hit you, is that what you're saying?

A. No, I saw it.

Q. Well, then, you must have seen whether I was stopped or not then, right?

A. Uh, no. I couldn't tell.

Q. Something was obstructing your vision from seeing my car?

A. No, I just didn't see, I guess. I wasn't paying that much attention. I just figured you'd stay there.

Q. Stay where?

A. In your lane.

Q. And as you approached the intersection, you weren't aware of me stopped or not?

A. No.

Q. And then suddenly I was out in the middle of the intersection?

A. That's about it.

Q. I must have accelerated fairly quickly?

A. You bet.

Q. And you saw it accelerate?

A. Yes, right out in front of me.

Q. You were watching my car that closely, and you couldn't tell if I was stopped or not?

A. Well, I really only started paying close attention when your car started accelerating.

Q. And you could tell it started accelerating because you were watching it?

A. Out of the corner of my eye.

Q. I take it you were watching the road out of the other corner?

Objection: Argumentative.

Judge: Sustained.

Q. What were you observing?

A. Well, everything. The road, the intersection, my driving.

A relatively tough witness. When you cross-examine, you aren't going to get an admission; you aren't going to destroy the witness, or necessarily get a glaring inconsistency. You have to work with what you get and argue the rest. All you want to do is try and create some lingering doubts, questions, and suspicions. In closing argument, you can develop these lingering suspicions into reasonable doubts. It totters on the edge of common sense that a person could witness so much yet witness so little. Emphasize proof beyond a reasonable doubt.

Immediate hazard

For violations including a right-of-way element, they'll also have to prove that the other driver was close enough when you were going through so as to constitute an *immediate hazard*. Whether the other car is an immediate hazard is another arguable issue, depending on the facts of each case. One interesting case held that evidence of a vehicle approaching an intersection at 40mph at a distance of 500-600 feet (approximately 1/10 of a mile) wasn't enough to prove it was an immediate hazard. *See* State v. Nicholson (12th District Court of Appeals, Preble County, June 23rd 1986). You requested discovery, got the driver's name and talked with him. He told you, among other things, that he was about 1/8 of a mile away from the intersection when he saw you pull into the intersection. At trial, you cross-examine the driver of the other vehicle, who was the only witness, besides you, to the incident.

Q. Sir, you say you were going the speed limit, right? (He has to admit this, for if he doesn't then he forfeits the right-of-way and you win)

A. Yes.

Q. The speed limit was 35mph?

A. Right.

Q. And you testified that you were going 30 to 35mph?

A. Yes.

Q. You saw me pull out into the intersection?

A. Yes, I did.

Q. Your honor, may the witness step down to the drawing board and make a sketch of the intersection? (He may have already done this during the prosecutor's questioning: he *should* have)

Judge: He may.

Q. (Witness goes to the board) Sir, if you could point out where you were when you first saw me?

A. (Points to place)

Q. Could you perhaps draw a vehicle there?

A. (Draws a vehicle)

Q. Thank you, and could you also draw where my vehicle was in the intersection.

A. (Draws your car in the intersection)

Q. Thank you sir, please take your seat.

A. (Witness goes back to witness stand)

Q. Now sir, you've said that you were approximately 1/8 of a mile from the intersection at that moment…the moment depicted in your diagram, right?

A. (If yes, then you've got a good case for closing argument) Uh, no, I said I was pretty close to the intersection.

Q. Sir, you never told me that you were approximately 1/8 of a mile away from the intersection when you first saw me in the intersection?

A. (If yes, you're golden) No. (What this means is you'll now have to take the stand as an '*impeachment* witness' [for the purposes of attacking the witness' credibility only]. You'll do this after the prosecution has rested its case)

Here's how. The prosecution, "Your honor, the state rests." You motion for a judgment of acquittal on various grounds. All grounds denied. You begin your 'case-in-chief.' You say, "Your honor, I would like to call myself to the stand for the *sole purpose of impeaching* the other driver's testimony. Specifically, I questioned him and asked him whether he had told me about the 1/8 of a mile distance before, and he denied this. I would like to take the stand as an impeachment witness only, regarding our previous discussion." Judge, "Well, you pretty much just did. But let's go ahead. You may take the stand." You take the oath and the stand and say (speaking to the judge or to the jury if there is one), "On the morning of January 21st I spoke with Mr. Joe Schmoe (the other driver) about this incident. I asked and he told me that when he first saw me in the intersection he was approximately 1/8 of a mile away." Judge, "Very well, would you like to now take the stand as a witness?" You, "No, your honor." Judge, "Very well, call your next witness." You step off the stand and complete your case-in-chief. If you have no other witnesses you say, "Your honor, the defense rests."

For your closing argument you want to focus on the facts of your case, how they show that his vehicle *didn't constitute an immediate hazard* to you. There is also a doubt as to what distance Joe Schmoe was away from the intersection. There in fact is a doubt with a reason behind it that he wasn't close enough to constitute an immediate hazard. Your testimony has him at 1/8 of a mile, you impeached him as telling you before that he was 1/8 of a mile away, and his testimony only states 'pretty close.' The *immediate hazard* element being one of the elements of the case that the prosecution must prove beyond a reasonable doubt, and there being a doubt with reason behind it as to his distance away so as to be an immediate hazard, they haven't produced sufficient solid evidence to convict you of the charge.

Forfeiture

Keep in mind that the other driver may *forfeit* the right-of-way. This is something you'll have to offer evidence to prove, either through cross-examination of the other driver, calling another witness of the incident or taking the stand yourself.

The other driver forfeits his right-of-way if he's not driving in a lawful manner. This can occur even if the driver is driving *within* the speed limit, because of §4511.21(A), which allows for a person to be driving unreasonably under the circumstances (and so in an unlawful manner) even if they're driving within the speed limit.

For example, imagine a winter day, slick roads and such, with the speed limit at 35mph. There is a four-way intersection with a flashing red stop signal in the direction you're going. You stop, look both ways, drive across, and slide, boom! He drives over the hill and hits you. You're a juvenile and your father was with you. You requested discovery and got a prior written statement by the other driver, saying he was driving 35mph (if he admitted to driving *over* the speed limit, then you win—because he forfeited the right-of-way; just ask in the preliminary motion that your case be dismissed for this reason, or file a motion to dismiss). You also find out, from the statement or calling and talking with him, that he is a local that drives through that area frequently. When the prosecution rests, and after you motion for a judgment of acquittal (and if the judge denies this motion), you call your dad to the stand as a witness for direct examination, "The defense calls Mr. J. B. A. Rockefeller IV to the stand."

Q. Good afternoon, Mr. Rockefeller, please state your full name for the record and spell it.

A. Jonathan Beauregard Alexander Rockefeller the fourth. It's spelt J…o…n…(judge: case dismissed!).

Q. What's your relation to me?

A. I'm your father.

Q. I'd like to draw your attention to the traffic incident I'm at trial here for today. Where were you at the time of the incident?

A. I was a passenger in your car, the car in the accident.

Q. Who else was in the car?

A. Only me and you.

Q. What were you doing?

A. Well, I had my seat belt on, and I was sitting there, watching the road ahead.

Q. What happened?

A. We came up to a red flashing light. You stopped the car and looked both ways. I did too, like I always do. There were no cars in sight. You then began driving across the intersection. While you were going through the intersection I glanced over and saw a car coming from my right. It was going at a fairly high rate of speed. I yelled for you to watch out, but it was too late. He clipped our back end.

Q. How fast would you say he was going?

A. I'd say about 40-45mph.

Q. Describe the roadway while looking to your right in the intersection.

A. Well, the road goes out about 100 feet and then drops off down a hill. So you can only see that 100 feet of road.

Q. What were the weather conditions that morning?

A. It was cold and snowing

Q. How about the road conditions?

A. The roads were slick and packed down with snow.

Q. Thank you. Your honor, I have no further questions at this time.

The prosecution will now cross-examine him. After they're done, you'll get another chance to ask him any questions regarding what the prosecutor cross-examined him on. Let's say you had previously cross-examined the other driver, after the prosecution had called him as a witness and questioned him (their direct examination of him), thusly.

Q. Sir, you live in the area?

A. Yes.

Q. And you've lived locally for how long?

A. For about five years.

Q. You've driven that road many times?

A. Yes, I have.

Q. How many times a week would you say?

A. About three times.

Q. And you've been doing this for five years?

A. Yes, thereabouts.

Q. Sir, you were driving fairly fast that morning, considering the road conditions, don't you think?

A. No, I was driving the speed limit.

Q. The roads were icy?

A. They had some snow on them.

Q. They were wet?

A. Yes.

Q. It was a cold morning?

A. Yes, relatively.

Q. Below freezing?

A. I assume. I don't know for sure.

Q. Yet you weren't driving below the speed limit?

A. Yes, I was.

Q. Well, the speed limit was 35mph, right?

A. Yes.

Q. And you were driving at least 35mph, right?

A. Probably about 30-35mph.

Q. Your honor, I have what's marked as defense exhibit 1 (with a sticker the court will provide you, or with your own) (Show the prosecutor the statement) It's the witness' prior statement, your honor. May I approach the witness?

Judge: You may.

Q. Sir, I'm showing you what's marked as defense exhibit 1, your prior statement. You recognize this as your statement?

A. Yes, that's my statement.

Q. Do you see where you wrote here, "I was going 35mph."?

A. Yes.

Q. (Walk back to where you were standing, keeping the statement) Now, you were also driving up a hill, right?

A. Yes.

Q. And so you had to keep pressing on the gas pedal to keep going that 35mph?

A. I guess.

Q. In other words, you had to keep *accelerating*, otherwise you wouldn't make it up the hill, or you'd slow down by the time you made it to the top?

A. I guess. In a sense.

Q. Maybe you accelerated back up to 35 mph *after* you got over the hill?

A. No. (If yes then you've got him accelerating up to a flashing yellow signal, for him, within 100 feet during lousy weather, et cetera, which is a great inconsistency)

Q. So you must have been going 35mph the entire time up the hill?

A. (If he says he *slowed down* to 35mph while going up the hill, then he was going *over* the speed limit, and so forfeits the right-of-way. If he says he *sped up* to 35mph, then you've got him, a person who is *very* familiar with the road and weather conditions, speeding up on his way up a hill to a flashing yellow signal) I guess so.

Q. But you knew a potentially dangerous intersection was just over the hill?

Objection: Asks for a conclusion.

Response (you): Your honor, this is based on his ample experience.

Judge: Ask a different question.

Q. You knew there was an intersection over the hill you were driving on?

A. Yes.

Q. You knew there was a flashing yellow signal for you?

A. Yes.

Q. You knew there was a flashing red signal for the other direction?

A. Yes. (If "No" to any of these questions then, "Sir, you've been driving this road three times a week for five years and you didn't know the traffic conditions at this intersection?")

Q. Yet you were going 35mph?

A. Yes.

That's *plenty* of ammunition for your closing argument. There are numerous doubts in the evidence that you can focus on during closing argument. Cover all of them thoroughly, but focus especially on the better ones. There's an old war dictum: the attacker, if attacking in ten different places, only has to win in one of them. Then the fortress is breached and the assault centers on this weakness like river water rushing to a crack in a dam.

Intention

Here's an important element for those cited under §4511.42–TL. The prosecution must prove beyond a reasonable doubt that you *intended* to turn left. They may do this using the officer's testimony. For instance, if after arriving on the scene you tell the officer you were getting ready to turn left, then they've got this element proved (the officer just has to testify to you telling him this at trial). Otherwise, the officer himself won't be able to establish that you intended to turn left.

Important Note: Hearsay

If the officer, while testifying, begins talking about what third persons said (people other than himself and you), then you should immediately stand and say, "Objection, your honor. Hearsay." For example, if the officer starts saying something like, "While I was on the scene the driver of the other car told me that the defendant was getting ready to turn left..." By the time the officer says, "told me," you should be standing and objecting. Remember, the officer can testify to what you told him, since you're the defendant. He is generally also allowed to testify as to what he said throughout his investigation, but possibly *only* what he said to *you*, so that when he gives your response it makes sense.

So if he gets carried away by saying stuff like, "I asked him (the third person) if the defendant was getting ready to turn left. After he answered I wrote the defendant a ticket for failure to yield the right of way while turning left." Well, that's bogus, because the officer's actions afterwards imply what the other driver told him. You should object to the court immediately, "Objection, your honor. The officer is phrasing his answers to imply an answer from the [third person]. This is all hearsay information." I know, I know, this is a lot of stuff to remember. Don't think you have to remember it all, just understand it, and if and when it comes up at trial you'll say, "Hey, wait a second, he can't do that."

Or they can have the other driver testify that you were in the turning lane, you were turning, or that he saw your blinker on, or some such nonsense. Possibly there are some skid marks that the officer reported and will testify to. This is all indirect (circumstantial) evidence of your intent to turn left, as opposed to you admitting it (direct evidence).

Lastly, for §4511.42–TL, they must show that the other vehicle was approaching from the opposite direction. If, say, the other vehicle was pulling out of the drive you were turning left into, and you collided, then he wasn't coming from the opposite direction. If you were cited under §4511.42 for such an incident, you were cited under the wrong law, and can file a Motion to Dismiss for a defect in the ticket as soon as possible. *See* Appendix on Forms, Motion to Dismiss.

Stop/Yield signs

In addition to all the possible inconsistencies mentioned above in the right-of-way section, to be properly cited under §4511.43(A)–TL for a stop sign violation, the other vehicle must already be in the intersection or approaching on *another* roadway. If the other driver is approaching from the opposite direction on the *same* roadway, then you've been improperly cited, unless they can show that he was *already* in the intersection. You can file a Motion to Dismiss. On cross-examination of the witness, you'll get evidence to show that he was *approaching* the intersection while you were in the intersection, or that he was stopped or yielding and hadn't entered the intersection yet by the time you were in the intersection.

Q. Where did our cars hit each other?

A. In the middle of the intersection.

Q. What part of the cars collided?

A. Let's see, you were turning left, so the right side of your front bumper (from the view of sitting in your car's drivers seat and looking out) and my front end.

Q. You were approaching from the opposite direction?

A. Yes.

Q. On the same road?

A. Yes.

Q. You say you saw my left turn signal was on?

A. Yes, I did.

Q. But you had legally stopped at the stop sign, like you're supposed to?

A. Yes, I always obey the traffic laws to a tee.

Q. And you say I then pulled out into the intersection to turn left?

A. Yes.

Q. You were planning on going straight ahead, and not turning?

A. Right.

Q. Then you did; you started from your stop and hit my car?

A. Well, our vehicles *collided* in the intersection. I didn't hit your car.

Q. And this occurred after you started from your stop and collided with my car, which was already in the intersection, right?

A. Right.

Now press this point during closing argument. Make sure during closing argument to read to the court the part of the statute that is applicable. Then highlight what the witness said during cross, focusing on this testimony placing doubt as to whether he was in the intersection.

Flashing yellow signals

The law provides that you may proceed, "only with caution." They must prove you didn't beyond a reasonable doubt. Even if there's an accident, if they don't produce a witness (or other evidence) that testifies with sufficient force to show you didn't proceed with caution, then you cannot be convicted.

Q. You were approaching the intersection from the opposite direction, right?

A. Yes.

Q. Now, as you approached, you noticed my car?

A. Yes, it was coming from the other direction.

Q. You say you saw my blinker on?

A. Yes.

Q. My left-turn blinker?

A. That's right.

Q. I came up to the intersection, right?

A. Yes.

Q. Slowed down before entering the intersection?

A. Yes, I noticed you slowing down.

Q. Then turned into the intersection?

A. Right.

Q. And that's when we collided, right?

A. Yes.

Q. I didn't swerve into you, right?

A. No.

Q. I didn't speed up to take the turn, did I?

A. No, you didn't. Like I said, you seemed to slow down. But you still hit me in the intersection.

Q. You didn't hear any wheels screeching?

A. No, nothing like that.

In this way you set the stage for arguing in closing that you were driving with caution, as is required. Furthermore, there is a doubt with reason behind hit, a reasonable doubt that what the prosecution says (you weren't exercising caution) is correct.

Stopping for school bus

All things being equal, you don't want this type of ticket. In the hearts and minds of most people, not stopping for a school bus equals running over young kids. It means more than just a speeding violation, it means not caring…so stop for school buses.

That being said, there are examples of absolutely ridiculous citations for this violation. A case example in point. One young man was pulled out of class, in front of his peers, and asked by the officer, "Do you know why I'm pulling you out of class?" The young man sincerely didn't. The officer said, "Because you didn't stop for a school bus. Do you know how dangerous that is?!" Turns out, the 'violation' had been committed more than a month before, and wasn't initially recorded by the bus driver—who happened to be a substitute for the usual driver. On some type of odd whim the bus driver decided to fill the complaint out. The young man really didn't know *what* the officer was talking about. The officer made the mistake of ticketing him, probably because of the general emotional outrage that is often associated with this type of ticket.

There are some interesting things about such a bus violation. First, a lot of people don't realize that you *don't* have to stop for a bus if it's a four (or more)-lane highway, and you're driving in the opposite direction of the bus (on the other side of the road). See §4511.75(C)–TL. I see it happen all the time, people stopping and clogging up traffic on the *other* side of the road from the bus. So please, if you're on the other side of a four or more-lane highway, do us a favor and don't stop.

The greatest obstacle to convicting you on such a charge is identity. Upon receiving notification of the alleged violation, the police officer is supposed to investigate to discover or confirm the identity of the operator of the vehicle. See §4511.751¶3–TL. If she can establish the identity of the operator, *then* she can issue a citation for this violation.

If, however, she *can't establish the identity* of the operator, then she can only issue a warning to the owner of the vehicle. What usually ends up happening is the officer will track down the owner using the license plate, ask some questions, and whoever the driver was will essentially say, "Yes, I was driving the vehicle from 10:00 to 10:45 (say the violation was at 10:15)." So the driver himself will pretty much *give* the prosecution this element. Let's say for example, that a bus driver takes down your plate number and a police officer comes to your door, asking, "Sir, are you the owner of…" "Were you driving your vehicle earlier this afternoon?" You respond, "I don't want to talk about it." He says in as stern a manner as he can muster, "Sir, there is a serious violation here, and we need some information from you; now, were you or weren't you driving your vehicle earlier today?" You respond calmly, "Sir, I don't want to talk about it." He says slyly, "About what?" You, "About anything." It could go on and on like this, you not saying anything except, "I don't want to talk about it." They can only issue you, or whoever the owner is, a warning. Not a ticket. Not a criminal charge. A *warning*. If they issue you anything else, you can motion to dismiss at arraignment or otherwise.

Now it may turn out (this is unlikely if you think about it) that the bus driver identifies you sufficiently in the report. First off, the bus driver's report isn't going to be what you might call a substantial repository of information. Secondly, the bus driver probably won't be able to identify you, unless you stick your head out of the car and wave and introduce yourself or some such crazy antics as that. He's sitting 100ft up in the air in his seat and your tucked way down in your seat underneath your hood. Also, you pass and he gets a look for a fleeting moment. This is why their reports won't sufficiently identify you.

Remember, if you didn't admit anything, and your ticket isn't dismissed, you can request this bus driver report through discovery. Also call the school bus coordinator to see if you can get a copy from them. Get a copy as soon as you can. It should be quite vague and fail to identify you adequately. You can motion to dismiss on these grounds. *See*

Appendix on Forms, Motion to Dismiss. You can motion to dismiss in your preliminary motions on trial day. At the end of the prosecutor's case, you may motion for a judgment of acquittal on these grounds—of failure to produce sufficient evidence to identify you as the operator of the vehicle at the time of the incident. Note in your closing argument to the court that a warning should have been given, as the appropriate law enforcement action, and cite and read the section to the court. See chapter four for an example on questioning someone about identity. Here's another cross-examination scenario of the bus driver:

Q. Sir, you were driving the bus on March 15th?

A. Yes, I was.

Q. You saw a vehicle pass by you?

A. Yes. I had my stop warning sign out, and then you passed my bus.

Q. You now know I own the car that passed you?

A. Yes.

Q. It's the car that passed you?

A. Definitely.

Q. So you say I passed you?

A. Yes, like I said, you passed me.

Q. Now, my car was passed from behind you, right?

A. Right.

Q. You first saw my car passing after you put your warning sign out?

A. Yes.

Q. And my car passed on your left, correct?

A. Yes, that's right.

Q. How did you get the license number?

A. Well, after you passed I got the license from you plate.

Q. Off the back of my car?

A. That's right.

Q. You didn't get the license off the front?

A. No.

Q. And all this took place in a matter of seconds, right?

A. Yes. (The conclusion is that he didn't have time to identify you. Leave this for closing argument, when you'll argue this point. If he didn't have time to do this he didn't have time to identify you either)

Q. (Next are the questions that depend on the driver's report) You filled out a report of this incident, didn't you?

A. Yes, I did. Later that day after I was done my shift.

Q. On the report you wrote down the license number?

A. Yes, we're required to.

Q. You described the car?

A. Yes I did.

Q. You say you followed the rules for filling this report out?

A. Of course I did.

Q. You're saying today under oath that you reported everything as you saw it as accurately as possible?

A. Yes *I did*. (If he thinks you're attacking his honor as a bus-report filler-outer, then he'll be emphatic about this. That's what you want. He may even perch himself higher up in the witness box when he says it. His only out is to say that he didn't fill out the report completely; he actually saw you real well, but didn't bother to write it down.)

Q. Sir, you didn't identify me in that report, did you?

A. (If "No," then you've won, and you can stop questioning) Yes, I did.

Q. Your honor, I have what is marked as defense exhibit 1. (This is the report) (The court will give you stickers to mark it with, or you can use your own) (Show the prosecutor the exhibit) May I approach the witness?

Judge: You may.

Q. (Show witness the report) Sir, I'm showing you what's marked as defense exhibit 1. You recognize this as your report?

A. Yes, I do.

Q. Look it over, and read where you say you identified me.

A. Here, I wrote "a white male."

Q. That's all the identifying characteristics you gave?

A. Yes.

Q. (Take the report back and walk to where you were standing) Sir, it's fair to say your report doesn't adequately identify me, isn't it?

Whatever he says, you don't need to argue with him. He might say, "Yeah, I think it does." Well, it doesn't matter what he thinks, only who's making the decision as to your guilt or innocence. You've sufficiently shown that he didn't adequately identify you, and you'll argue this extensively in your closing argument. You'll first motion for a judgment of acquittal for a second time after your 'case-in-chief,' on the grounds of insufficient evidence to identify you as the operator of the vehicle.

By the way, you don't have to take the stand. It's your right not to, and it can't be held against you. Some traffic ticket defense books recommend that you take the stand as a witness in your own defense, on the grounds that the judge will naturally think that you did *something* to get this ticket, so you better defend yourself. Now that's damned *infuriating!* What that author is saying is that you're guilty unless you prove yourself innocent. What that author does is attack the integrity of judges and/or juries, implying that they can't abide by the *constitutional requirement* that the fact that you don't take the stand *can't* be held against you. Remember, always remember, **they have to prove you guilty beyond a reasonable doubt,** whether you take the stand or not.

Street/Drag racing

First of all, if the citation on your ticket reads 4511.251(A), then you can motion to dismiss at your arraignment or soon thereafter. To get you for street racing, they have to cite you under 4511.251*(B).* Subsection (A) just defines what street racing is; it doesn't *prohibit* it. If the prosecution motions to amend your ticket to include section 4511.251(B), object, "Your honor, I object. This amendment would change the nature and identity of the crime charged against me, and so is not allowed."

Among other things, the prosecution must show *intent* on your part to outdistance another vehicle. They must show this was a *competitive* intent, as opposed to say, just intent to overtake or pass another vehicle. *See* State v. Barrett, 340 N.E.2d 418. If a person is next to you and you accelerate to pass him, and then he gets wise and accelerates to prevent this (for whatever reason) and so on and so forth—Well, when you get pulled over and cited under this section, be thankful. It's not going to be easy for them to show this intent. Their best chance of winning might in fact come *if* and when you take the stand. They'll twist you and turn you and get it out of you. You don't have to take the stand. Make them prove it, find inconsistencies, argue in closing argument that they didn't prove competitive intent beyond a reasonable doubt.

Look back at the last sentence of §4511.251(A). This is an important sentence. What it says is that if both you and the other guy are traveling side by side at speeds greater than the prima facie (presumed) speed limit, *or* if you both *rapidly* accelerate from a *common* starting point to speeds in excess of the prima facie speed limit on the road, then either of these situations will be *all the prosecution has to show* in order to prove you were street racing (including showing the intent element above). You can offer evidence to combat this proof. For instance, you might get the officer to say you weren't *rapidly* accelerating, or to say things that will allow you to argue this point in closing argument. For instance, the officer may testify to there being no screeching of wheels, no smoke from contact between the tires and the road, that your car traveled a substantial distance to get to the prima facie speed (say a quarter mile to get to a speed of 35mph: use your physics book), or a number of other indications. These types of facts create reasonable doubts as to the element of rapidity.

Street racing is a six-point violation. That's steep, because *real* drag racing is a little dangerous. No, hold on…it's a *lot* dangerous, for you and other people. I'm not talking about that chumpy zero to forty you and your friends do. So if you get a street racing ticket based on this chumpy type of racing, you might request a reduction in sentence to, say, a driving without reasonable control or a straight speeding ticket, which are both generally two-point violations. Just tell the prosecutor that you know you're a chump, and it wasn't *real* drag racing anyway. Maybe you'll get lucky.

Switching lanes

There's a case-story involving switching lanes that serves to teach two important lessons I've been stressing on and off throughout this book.

First, you should be wary to take the stand, unless you've *really* got your story down, and have considered where the prosecutor may cross-examine you and how you'll effectively respond. The story also teaches the importance of carefully looking at the law you were cited under and ensuring that you were cited under the *correct* one.

A young man was cited under §4511.33(A)–T, which concerns driving in marked lanes. A police cruiser was traveling about 100 yards behind him on a four-lane highway (two lanes each direction, separated by a median). There were a few cars interspersed between them. The officer noticed the car moving from one lane to the other once, then back again, and then again for a third time. According to the officer, it sort of 'swerved' from one lane to the next, no blinker was ever used, and a car behind the swerving car applied its brakes, apparently to avoid the swerving car. He pulled the young man over and gave him a ticket. At arraignment and pre-trial the plea was, "Not true." So trial was set.

Lesson as to the citation

The officer should have cited the young man under §4511.39¶1–TL, which prohibits movement on a highway without, among other things, "giving an appropriate signal." The officer's testimony focused almost completely on the juvenile's failure to use his signals before changing lanes. This *isn't enough* to show that the young man didn't "first ascertain that such movement could be made with safety," proof of which is required for conviction under §4511.33(A), which is, again, what the officer cited the young man under. That's clear enough—I've often changed lanes without using my blinkers, but *only* after first looking in my rear view mirrors to ensure that it's safe to do so. This activity isn't a violation of §4511.33(A). If the juvenile was aware of this defect, he could have motioned for a dismissal, either at his arraignment, pre-trial, or by filing one with the clerk of courts and the prosecutor. Or after the prosecution was done presenting his case-in-chief, he could have motioned for a judgment of acquittal based on insufficiency of evidence. He had all kinds of promising options…that he was probably unaware of. But this is what he did.

Lesson as to testifying on your own behalf

He took the stand, which he didn't have to do. He offered the following defense, which he didn't have to do. His brother, who was in the car with him, kept "hitting and pushing" him. *That's* what made him swerve from one lane to the next. A straightforward, simple defense: He wasn't at fault; his brother interfered with his ability to keep his car on a straight path. He told the police officer this at the time, but the officer still cited him, when he should've cited his *brother!* Sounds good, doesn't it? Cross-examination.

Q. You say your brother pushed you?

A. Yes, he did.

Q. On your arm and shoulder, here? (Showing part of right arm and shoulder)

A. Yes, in that area.

Q. You didn't see it coming, did you?

A. No, he was laughing and then suddenly pushed me.

Q. The first time?

A. Each time, but yeah the first time too.

Q. And you, your car, then moved into the other lane?

A. Yes.

Q. Each time he pushed you?

A. Yes.

Q. You didn't have time to react because it happened so fast?

A. No, I really didn't.

Q. He pushed...you swerved?

A. Right.

Q. He pushed you just as hard each time?

A. Yes, he did.

Q. And he pushed you in the same manner, like this? (Demonstrating)

A. Yes, like that. (Demonstrates himself)

Q. Each time?

A. Yes.

Q. You were just going about your business, watching the road in front of you, and then he did this, right?

A. Yes, that's right.

Q. He didn't even give you a chance to see if it was clear, did he?

A. No, he just did it…pushed me, and the car went over. But after I was over there, I stayed in the lane. I didn't swerve around or anything like the officer said I did.

He essentially admits that he in no way looked to see if he could switch lanes with safety. What about his defense? His answer to the last question gives the solution.

Q. You didn't swerve like the officer said?

A. No.

Q. You drove as good as you could…under the circumstances, right?

A. Yes.

Q. And stayed in your lane?

A. Yes, but I couldn't help it when my brother pushed me. I told him to stop.

Q. But he didn't?

A. No, he didn't.

Q. When did you tell him to stop, after the first time?

A. Yes, each time he did it.

Q. So, the first time…he pushed you, the car went into the other lane. You stayed in that lane and told him not to do it again, right?

A. That's right.

Q. But he did…do it again. He pushed you like this? (Demonstrates)

A. Yes.

Q. And then you went back into the lane where you had started?

A. Yes, because he pushed me.

Q. And you stayed in that lane and told him to stop, right?

A. Right.

Q. And didn't' swerve?

A. Not at all.

Q. Did that happen again?

A. Yes, I think it happened three or four times total.

Q. The same way?

A. Yes.

Q. Your honor, if the witness could step down so we could do a demonstration?

Magistrate: Sure.

Q. Mr. X, please step down and let's do a demonstration for the magistrate of how your brother pushed you, okay?

A. All right.

The prosecutor sets up two chairs facing the magistrate. The prosecutor acts as the defendant driver; the defendant acts as his brother in the passenger seat.

Q. Show us how he pushed you.

A. Like this (Pushes prosecutor's arm and shoulder away from him)

Q. Then you went into the other lane, like this? (Prosecutor shows himself turning as if moving to the left)

A. Right.

Q. Now, show us the next time.

A. He did the same thing after I told him not to, like this.

Q. Then you went into the other lane like this? (Prosecutor shows same movement)

A. Yes.

Q. Now show us the next time.

A. (Pushes prosecutor)

Q. You went like this again, right?

A. Yes.

Q. And again maybe one more time?

A. Yes, maybe one more time. But he pushed me each time even though I told him not to.

Q. Just like this?

A. Yes.

Q. Okay, thank you. Please take your seat again.

A. (Takes his seat at the witness stand)

Q. That's not smart, what your brother did. What lane did you start in?

A. It was the right lane.

Q. He pushed you, and you swerved to the left lane?

A. Yes.

Q. You stayed there and told him to stop, but he pushed you again?

A. Yes.

Q. And then, because he pushed you again like you showed us, you went to your left like you showed us…into the third lane?

A. (No response. The part of the freeway he was on only had two lanes)

Q. Did you hear my question?

A.…Well, no.

Q. When he pushed you the second time, you didn't go into the third lane, because there is no third lane, is there?

A. No.

Q. You didn't run over the median?

A. No.

Q. How about a guardrail?

A. No, I swerved back into the right lane.

Q. Now, young man, we just went over the whole scenario. You came down here and gave a demonstration to the judge, under oath. She was watching you. You showed her how your brother *pushed* you each time, and how the car moved to the left each time after he pushed you. How you steered to the left. Are you now saying that's not what happened?

A. …I don't know. I just went into the right lane.

Q. Even though your brother pushed you and your steering wheel turned left?

A. …I don't know.

Q. You don't know if your car went right even though you turned it left?

A. ...No... I'm not sure. I just went into the right lane after.

Q. And this happened more than once, since you showed us how your brother pushed you and how you turned left, and said this happened maybe four times, right?

A. (No response)

Q. Did you hear my question?

A. Yes.

Q. But you can't answer it, can you?

A. ...No. I don't know.

His defense is ruined, and so is his credibility. Before, if he wouldn't have taken the stand, he had a strong argument that the government didn't provide sufficient evidence to prove beyond a reasonable doubt that he didn't check first to see if he could make the lane change with safety. Now, by taking the stand, he's admitted to not looking and his credibility is shot. That's an example of what can happen to you if you decide to take the stand and you don't have your story straight. Whether you're *really* telling the truth or not is irrelevant *as far as this* is concerned, because if you don't have your story straight, even though you may be telling the truth, and the prosecution tears your story apart, then you'll *look like* you're not telling the truth...and in this instance, *perception is reality*, so to speak.

Reckless v. Reasonable

§4511.20&201 violations are frequently referred to as *reckless* operation (reck-op). Reck-ops are a four-point offense. §4511.202 violations are referred to as *without reasonable control* (WRC) operation. WRC is a two-point offence. Both reck-op and WRC are a first time minor misdemeanor. If you've received a reck-op, *and* you've run out of options for fighting it, then you might try and get it reduced to a WRC viola-tion. The prosecutor will often agree to this because a reck-op is much more difficult to prove than a WRC. Here's why.

First, as an example, say you drive your car into a ditch. On this fact alone, without any other evidence or witnesses, you can be convicted of a WRC. But you can't be convicted of a reck-op on this evidence alone. *See* State v. Flagge, (4th District Court of Appeals, Adams County, April 12, 1993). Generally, the fact that there's an accident isn't enough evi-dence to prove you guilty of a reck-op. The prosecution can't just bring the officer, who wasn't a witness to the accident, to the stand and have him testify as to the weather conditions, skid marks on the road, and other circumstances, and hope to convict you of a reck-op. *See* City of Columbus v. Amarine, 201 N.E.2d 915 (Remember, 201 is the volume, N.E.2d is the book, and 915 is the page number: ask your local law librarian). Evidence of speeding is not enough either. All of this *may* be sufficient evidence to prove you guilty of a *WRC*, but not a reck-op. If this is all the evidence they provide, and they don't have a *witness to the incident* testify sufficiently to your driving, then you can motion for a judgment of acquittal at the end of the prosecutor's case, on these grounds. "Your honor, I motion for acquittal on the basis of an insuffi-ciency of evidence. In particular, the prosecution didn't sufficiently establish that I was driving recklessly. They only provided evidence from the police officer, who was not a witness to the accident, of the weather conditions, marks on the road, and such.".

Also, for a reck-op, the prosecution has to show that you acted willfully or wantonly. They have to show this, as all other material elements, beyond a reasonable doubt. Here's the definition of *reckless*:

§2901.22(C)

A person acts recklessly when, with heedless indifference to the conse-quences, he perversely disregards a known risk that his conduct is likely to cause a certain result or is likely to be of a certain nature. A person is reckless with respect to circumstances when, with heedless indifference to the consequences, her perversely disregards a known risk that such circumstances are likely to exist.

This seems to correspond to what we might think of as *wanton*? Willful seems to correspond to a *higher* state of culpability, like knowledge or purpose. Indeed, under the so-called Model Penal Code, 'willfully' is satisfied if a person acts *knowingly* with respect to the material elements of the charge. *See* M.P.C. §2.02(8). In fact, the *United States Supreme Court* says that an act is willfully done, if done voluntarily or intentionally and with the specific intent to fail to do something the law requires to be done…with bad purpose either to disobey or disregard the law. *See* Screws v. United States, 325 U.S. 91.

Blacks Law Dictionary defines willfully as "Proceeding from a conscious motion of the will; voluntary; knowingly; deliberate. Intending the result which actually comes to pass; designed; intentional; purposeful; not accidental or involuntary." It seems evident that the willfulness standard is thus *higher* than the wantonness standard.

Why's this so important? There's a case that says that since *two* mental states are established for one criminal act (in §4511.20 or .201), the prosecution bears the burden of establishing the "greater degree of culpability, *willfulness,* beyond a reasonable doubt." *See* State v. Earlenbaugh, 479 N.E.2d 846 (italics added).

They have to do it beyond a reasonable doubt. They'll need witnesses, good witnesses. A witness that takes the stand and says you didn't intend to do it, you didn't know it was going to happen, you tried to *avoid* it rather than do it, or anything at all that alludes to the action not being deliberate, intentional, *willful,* is a *good* witness for you, even if they were called by the prosecution to testify against you. What's more, if the witness is just a witness *to the accident,* and not to *you* and how you acted (showing *your* mental state), then they'll have considerable trouble establishing your mental state of willfulness. You must motion for a judgment of acquittal based on the insufficiency of evidence for proving the mental state of willfulness beyond a reasonable doubt. One of the easiest ways to prove this intent element is if you take the stand and get yourself in a bind. Remember, it's your constitutional right not to take the stand.

VASCAR

The prosecution better have the officer testify as to the precise distance you were timed over. It better be accurate. If not, then there's no way your measured speed can be accurate. If the officer used his odometer to measure the distance, but doesn't testify to its accuracy, or of having it checked to make sure it was accurately measuring distance, then you can motion for a judgment of acquittal based on these grounds. VASCAR and stopwatches are prone to human error. Consider a measured distance of 1000 feet. The officer is sitting at the 1000 foot marker, and begins timing when she *sees* you cross the 0 foot line. What if you were only 900-950 feet away? The recorded speed will be higher.

If the facts of your case are right, consider questioning the officer on her observation of your vehicle—the weather conditions, curves in the road, other passing cars or cars in front of you, and other possible obstructions to her view.

Aerial observation (Pennsylvania turnpike)

I'm experienced in this type of traffic ticket. I think I told you why, right? Once I defended a case for 87mph in a 65mph on the PA turnpike. What a great defendant too, did everything I asked of him, showed up on time, always had great input. If you haven't figured it out, the defendant was yours truly. I'm not a hotshot—I just like golf. I *really* wasn't going that speed. Honest—I was actually going faster. Shows how good their detectors are. By the way, for those of you out there (and

I'm sure you're out there), that's *not* a defense, "Your honor, they cited the *wrong* speed limit on my ticket. I wasn't going 87mph. I was actually going 105mph."

Anyway, to make a short story long, I was rolling down the turnpike, and rightly so, since I was going golfing. My radar detector was on. A ways up I came over a hill, and then I saw them: two squad cars sitting on the side. I decelerated to about 75mph, and then passed. One pulled out and put his flashers on. I was stunned. Why didn't my lousy radar pick him up? The officer came to the window, and said, "Sir, may I see your driver license and registration?" Sure. Then he said the old, "Did you know this is a 65mph speed zone?" Yes. "Did you know that you were going 87?"...No. "How fast were you going?" The speed limit. (Yeah, the speed limit on the Audubon, but nonetheless the speed limit). I still couldn't figure out why my radar detector hadn't worked. I asked, "What's the ticket for?" He said, "You were tracked by aerial observation going 87mph." I said, "You mean a *helicopter*?" I was relieved my radar detector hadn't failed me.

"Yes, sir," he said. He went back to his car, came back and gave me the ticket. I noticed there was a mark through the radar box (as if he had used a radar), but there was a circle around it. There was also a mark through the aerial observation box. I pointed to the radar box and asked, "I thought you said you didn't use radar?" He said, "I marked it by mistake. You see I crossed it out." "So where do I plead not guilty?" "It's all on the back of your ticket, sir."

All right. First, *always* look to Chapter 12 and make a checklist of all those requirements they have to meet at trial. At my trial, they didn't meet *any* of them, and the judge dismissed the case on his own motion. If they don't meet these requirements, then you must motion for a judgment of acquittal. *See* Practice Section.

The alleged helicopter-officer wasn't at the trial. The officer that pulled me over began testifying,

Officer. On [such and such a date] Officer X relayed to me…

Me. May I object your honor?

Judge. On what grounds?

Me. Hearsay.

Judge. Sustained.

What happened was the officer immediately began telling the judge about what the *other officer* told him. You can stop him from doing this. It's hearsay. But if you don't object, he'll go right on ahead and keep talking and get all that information in. The very fact that the helo-officer wasn't present meant my case was going to get thrown out as long as I objected on hearsay grounds. The officer continued,

Officer. I pulled him over. I knew it was him because…

Me. Objection, your honor. Hearsay (He was about to say how the other officer identified my car)

Judge. Sustained.

Officer. I cited him for 87mph in the 65mph zone.

He said a few other things, but that was pretty much it. The state rests. They didn't establish venue. They didn't establish identity. They didn't introduce the certificate of accuracy. They didn't introduce evidence showing it was a Department of Transportation (DOT) approved device that timed me. They didn't introduce evidence showing it was a DOT approved station that tested and issued the certificate of accuracy for the device (that they didn't introduce anyway). We didn't even know what type of device was used. I then asked the judge if I could see the certificate of accuracy. The officer had to go get a fax of it (i.e. not the original). And the state had already rested, so there was no way for them to authenticate this copy (prove that it was an accurate copy of the original, which they have to do. There was no appropriate seal on the certificate, which might allow them to introduce the certificate. It was after all, a *copy*). *See* Chapter 12 for discussion of these topics.

Further, the officer had marked two boxes, for radar and aerial observation, on the ticket (something I never got a chance to bring up). I could have cross-examined him on this point, but they had left so much procedure out of their case, that it became a trivial addition. I also noticed on the ticket that the electronic stopwatch purportedly used was allegedly tested that morning at 8:00 A.M. Thinking this dubious, I intended to cross-examine the helo-officer on his activities that morning to get him to give his activities up to the moment he boarded the helicopter. Then I would return back to the testing time, and have him stumble over the fact that he 'forgot' to mention he had done this too (but he didn't show up for trial). The improper check mark in the radar box and the testing time of the electronic box were my only *substantive* arguments. All the rest were procedural. I was hoping that, if they met all their procedural requirements, I would be able to raise enough inconsistency from these two potential substantive weaknesses to produce a reasonable doubt as to my speeding. That was my plan: Plan and hope for a procedural goof up, and be on the constant look out for one (You only need one; attack in ten places, win in one), with the fallback position of creating a reasonable doubt based on the two substantive issues. I *didn't* have much (I didn't have the slightest idea how good they were at meeting their procedural requirements, and I didn't want to ask or in any way tip my hand that this was my strategy, and so didn't get in touch with them or make any discovery requests through a strategic choice), and *I* went for it. It's not that difficult. It just requires work.

The judge dismissed the ticket because of the failure concerning the certificate of accuracy, before I even had a chance to motion for a judgment of acquittal, which is when I would have brought all these other requirements up and discussed how the prosecution didn't meet them.

The judge also reprimanded the officer for not having the other officer at trial, noting that the case might have been a lot easier had he done so. Doubtful.

Because I was prepared. I only discovered all these requirements because *I used the method I'm telling you about in this book.* It *required* work, yes. (It turns out, if you call the PA Turnpike Commission, you can go down and look at their list of regulations. If you did, you'd discover all these things I'm mentioning. In fact, each toll plaza *must* have a copy of them). It was work, but it paid off. My ticket was dismissed, and more importantly I learned a great deal about the law. That's important, because we're the only ones who can hold the government's feet to the fire when it comes to the law. We have to make sure they're abiding by it. Other people had pled not guilty and were having their similar cases heard just prior to mine. I listened, and more often than not the only thing they were looking for was a *break*. They hadn't done their research. They hadn't prepared. They didn't really *care*, and the judge could tell (as they always can). The judge, in fact, complemented me on the work I did. That was the best part of the experience, believe it or not. He was a good judge, and they often are. They're fair, and they do give you the benefit of the doubt. If you're professional, confident and sincere, they'll listen to you. If you've done your homework and have a good argument, you've got a good chance.

RADAR

RAdio Detection And Ranging. That's where the acronym comes from. You've seen the things the prosecution must show. *See* Chapter 11. You can *request production* of the officer's *calibration and/or traffic log* at trial. *See* State v. McCann, (Fifth District Court of Appeals, Licking County, July 23, 1993). This will allow you to see if in fact, among other things, the officer internally and externally calibrated the radar before and after her shift. You can also request discovery on the radar *owner/operators manual*, or request its production at trial. That way, you can see what procedures are required for testing and calibration, as well as maintenance and the radars susceptibility to external interference (such as snow, rain, fog, or other electromagnetic sources). The radar should also have a *maintenance log*, which you can request discovery or production on. The law enforcement department may have its own maintenance (or other) manual.

You should have a checklist with what the prosecution has to prove. While the officer is on the stand, make sure they cover each of these areas. If they don't, then when the prosecution rests you'll motion for a judgment of acquittal based on this.

For instance, say that the officer didn't testify as to his qualifications for use of the radar (element (3) in chapter 11). The prosecution rests. You stand and say, "Your honor, I motion for acquittal. The prosecution didn't offer any evidence showing the officer's qualifications for operating the radar. As this is required of them to show, and they failed to do so, I motion for acquittal." Or, lets say that the officer testified to all of these things except the radars audio monitor (element (4)c. in chapter 11). You motion for a judgment of acquittal, "Your honor, I motion for a judgment of acquittal. The prosecution offered no evidence that the radar's *audio* monitor corroborated his visual identification and the radar's visual speed display. Evidence as to the audio monitor's reading is required to prove the officer used the radar unit properly, and must be shown in order to secure a conviction for speeding when using radar. Since they didn't do this, I motion for a judgment of acquittal."

Keep in mind you wouldn't cross-examine them as to these things. If, say, the officer doesn't testify to externally calibrating the radar (element (2)b.ii. in chapter 11), don't ask him, after the prosecutor is done questioning, "So, you didn't externally calibrate the radar, did you?" Because now he simply testifies to it, and this requirement is established. Or, say, you got the owner/operators manual through discovery, and the officer's testimony differs from the calibration requirements in the operator's manual, then you motion for a judgment of acquittal on those grounds (Only if there's a flagrant difference between the operator's manual and the officer's testimony should you bring it up on cross—a difference you know he won't be able to correct). Just make a checklist of all these requirements, and ensure the prosecution adequately covers them. If they're not, you can motion for a judgment of acquittal.

What do you cross-examine a police officer on, then? Well, first of all, when you do cross-examine a police officer, here are some tips. Always be professional; always be courteous. Don't argue with the officer or raise your voice. The judge or magistrate often knows the officer, or knows about the officer. They never take too kindly to officers being lambasted on the witness stand. This can only hurt your case, sometimes seriously. But don't get me wrong. You should be this way with *all* witnesses you cross-examine. Officers shouldn't be given any special consideration. They're fair game. They're just as likely as anyone else to confuse facts, forget incidents, be irresponsible, bend the truth or flat out conceal it. Furthermore, to dispel a common myth, they're not somehow specially trained or suited for testifying at trial. Most have very little experience at it. A good cross-examination will reveal inconsistencies in their stories just as easily as a good cross-examination will reveal them in any other person's. What's important is that since the officer's testimony is often given much more weight than your every day Joe Blow, once an inconsistency in the officer's testimony *is* discovered and rooted out, it will hurt the prosecution's case doubly, no...*trebly*.

Perhaps a better word is *terribly*. It turns out that police officer's are frequently *better* targets for cross-examination, for they're often proud and so susceptible to hyperbole. Perhaps a better word is *exaggeration*— exaggeration of their perceptive abilities, of their law enforcement capabilities, or the precision of their methods. Prepare a strong, pointed and in depth cross-examination of critical potential weak points, and incon-sistencies are sure to follow.

You can cross-examine the officer on such things as,

1 The amount of traffic around your car when his radar was activated.
2 If he had his radar on automatic (which indicates that he was-n't actually pointing the radar at you specifically, and so could've been detecting another vehicle's movement).
3 The steadiness of the speed of his vehicle.
4 The officer's competence to use the radar unit. For instance, his training on this type of radar, or his general knowledge about radar principles (which he should have learned during his training).
5 The external environment, including nearby parked vehicles, buildings, street signs, weather conditions (especially sleet, snow and rain), and any other circumstances potentially inter-fering with the radar's accuracy.
6 Particular interference effects that may be applicable, such as:
   a. *Cosine*: This is a directional error, and concerns the angle between the radar antenna (and so the path of the radia-tion) and your vehicle. The greater the angle the worse the readout. Typically, law enforcement departments want no more than a five-degree angle.
   b. *Multiple reflection*: This error occurs when large external objects such as buildings, bridges or signs (including over-head signs) or other moving cars produce radar reflections into the antenna, creating cosine effects.
   c. *Shadowing*: Usually occurs when your vehicle is moving towards the police vehicle, but there's another larger vehicle that has passed the police vehicle, and is moving away from

it at a slow speed. The radar will add your speed and the other vehicle's speed, and display this as your speed.

    d. Numerous other possible interference effects that you may find discussed in the operator's manual (some radars are more susceptible to certain types of interference than others) or in a book on radars at your local library.

7 If you received his calibration log, and he didn't log the radar calibration.

8 If you received his traffic log and he didn't properly log your traffic stop.

9 If you received the radars owner/operators manual and there is a substantial difference between its requirements and the officer's testimony.

10 If you received the law enforcement department's policy on radar citations and there is a difference between these and the officer's testimony.

Let's take some case examples.

Factual Scenario #1

Let's say the police officer radars you speeding. Pulls you over...gives you a ticket. Repeats process with another victim-driver. At the end of her shift, she calibrates the radar she used that day for her devious deeds. She does both the internal and external calibrations, but she doesn't record having done so in her calibration log book. Further, the law enforcement department she works with has a policy requiring calibration logs. You request discovery and receive both the calibration log and the policy manual (Perhaps you requested and the prosecutor denied; then file a Motion for Discovery; you may also motion for production of these documents at trial, and ask the judge for a reasonable amount of time to look these over to see if in fact there are some omissions). Regardless, you discover that she didn't include any documentation of having done calibration tests *after* ticketing you, though she did include calibration tests for before.

When the prosecutor calls her to the stand as a witness, which he'll have to do, she testifies to calibrating the radar both before and after her shift. You cross-examine:

Q. Ma'am, you've worked for the Dunkin law department for ten years? (She testified to this on her direct examination with the prosecutor)

A. Yes, I have.

Q. And you've worked traffic law enforcement there for eight of those ten years?

A. Yes.

Q. And before you began working for the Dunkin law department you received training?

A. Yes, at the academy. And I have an undergraduate in criminal justice.

Q. You're aware of the department's policy on traffic ticketing, correct?

A. Yes.

Q. Does the department ever have classes on it…instruction and what not?

A. Well, every six months or so they have a refresher course, but that's about all.

Q. But part of your job is to *know* this policy?

A. Yes.

Q. And to apply it properly?

A. Yes, of course.

Q. This is so because if you don't, there may be a risk that innocent people will be ticketed?

A. I guess.

Q. The law department's reason for this policy manual is to give
you guidelines?

A. Yes.

Q. Some mandatory perhaps, some advisory?

A. Yes, perhaps.

Q. And the mandatory ones, you'd consider them more important?

A. Well, not necessarily. The advisory parts could be just as
important, depending on the situation.

Q. But if they're mandatory, they you must abide by them, right?

A. Yes.

Q. It's fair to say then, that *someone* thought them fairly important to make mandatory?

A. Right.

Q. To guide you in your public service to the community, right?

A. Right.

Q. You haven't taken this refresher course as of late, have you?

A. (If no, it's good for you because she should have; if yes, it's
good for you because she didn't follow it; if there aren't refresher
courses, it's good for you because even more so she must maintain knowledge of the policy) No.

Q. The last time was when?

A. About two years ago.

Q. The refresher course isn't mandatory?

A. Every two years.

Q. So you'll have to take it soon?

A. Yes.

Q. Now, part of your department's policy, recorded in this manual, is that you *must* calibrate your radar?

A. Yes.

Q. That's mandatory?

A. Yes.

Q. Also, you must record calibrating your radar?

A. Yes, that's right.

Q. And that's mandatory too?

A. I believe so.

Q. The department's policy requires that you log your calibrations, right?

A. I believe so.

Q. Your honor, I have what's marked as defense exhibit 1 (The applicable portion of the law department policy). (Show the prosecutor) May I approach the witness?

Prosecutor. Your honor, if I may ask, for what purposes?

Judge. What for?

You. Your honor, the officer said she *believes* that the policy is she must record her calibrations. I want to have her view the policy to clarify for the record that she *must* record these calibrations. (So introducing this record would be unnecessary if the officer admits that recording the calibration is required)

Judge. Very well, you may approach.

Q. Ma'am, I'm showing you a copy of defense exhibit 1. Do you recognize this?

A. Yes, I do.

Q. What is it?

A. It's part of the police department's policy on traffic enforcement.

Q. I'm going to read a portion of this policy to you, right here. (Show and point to portion so she can follow along) It says, *All radars used in traffic enforcement shall be calibrated before and after each shift. These calibrations **shall be** logged in the officer's calibration logbook.* Did I read that correctly, ma'am?

A. Yes.

Q. (Now you can move on; Step back to where you were standing, taking the policy manual with you) Ma'am, as you testified to earlier, you have to do both internal and external calibration tests? (The radar/laser manual will specify what tests must be done; the department's policy manual should also)

A. Yes.

Q. Then record them?

A. Yes.

Q. On the morning of January 1st (The day you received your ticket) you calibrated your radar?

A. Yes, I did.

Q. Naturally, you recorded this calibration?

A. Yes, that's what I do.

Q. When you calibrate your radar?

A. Yes.

Q. Because it's what the policy manual requires?

A. Right.

Q. But, on January 1st, despite it being required, you didn't record any type of calibration *after* your shift, did you?

If A. No, then

Q. But you're required to do this, right?

A. Yes.

Q. And it's "what you do," as you said ma'am, when you've *actually done* a calibration?

A. Yes.

Q. So the natural conclusion, from your calibration log, is that you didn't do any calibration checks after your shift, right?

A. Well, I *did* do them. I must have forgotten to record it.

Q. Ma'am, looking at the calibration log the natural conclusion, considering that it's "what you do," and it's a department requirement…the natural conclusion would be that you didn't do any calibration checks after your shift, right?

A. I'm not sure if it's a natural conclusion…(Avoidance)

Q. It's certainly a *reasonable* one?

A. I suppose. (So you've got a reasonable doubt here, generated from this inconsistency)

If A. Yes I did, then

Q. Your honor, I have what is marked as exhibit 2. (Show the prosecution, markings can be done with little stickers, but the court will provide you with some if you ask; it's very straightforward) May I approach the witness?

Judge. You may.

Q. Ma'am, I'm showing you what's marked as exhibit 2. Do you recognize this?

A. Yes.

Q. What is it?

A. It's my calibration log.

Q. You see the date on the top of this page in your calibration log?

A. Yes, it's January 1st.

Q. The day of this incident.

A. Yes.

Q. (Give the officer the logbook) Ma'am, point out where in the logbook you did calibrations *before* your shift.

A. (Points to them) Right here, it's marked as done at 8 A.M.

Q. Now, if you would ma'am, find the mandatory entries that show you did calibration checks *after* your shift.

A. (Looks over the logbook) There aren't any…but I did them.

Q. There's no record of having done any calibration checks after your shift?

A. No.

Q. (Take logbook back, and go back to where you were standing) But you're required to do this, right?

A. Yes.

Q. And it's "what you do," as you said ma'am, when you've *actually done* a calibration?

A. Yes.

Q. So the natural conclusion, from your calibration log, is that you didn't do any calibration checks after your shift, right?

A. Well, I *did* do them. I must have forgotten to record it.

Q. Ma'am, looking at the calibration log the natural conclusion, considering that it's "what you do," and it's a department requirement…the natural conclusion would be that you didn't do any calibration checks after your shift, right?

A. I'm not sure if that's a *natural* conclusion…(Avoidance)

Q. It's certainly a *reasonable* one?

A. Not after listening to my testimony it wouldn't be.

Q. What if you hadn't logged *any* calibration checks, or, say, hadn't written down the speed I was going *on the ticket*, but you testified to it—that would be all right too?

A. Well, I *did* the calibration checks.

Q. Ma'am, could you please answer the question.

A. Well, I'm not sure.

Q. Even though you failed to do something you're *required* to do?

A. Well, I suppose.

Q. And you're required to do these things because as a public servant, you must ensure that you don't ticket innocent people?

A. Well, I do them to protect the public, yes.

Q. But in this case you didn't, did you?

A. Yes, I protected the public.

Q. But you didn't do what was required of you, did you?

You have excellent ammo here. First, you'll motion for a judgment of acquittal when the prosecution rests. You'll stand and say, "Your honor, I motion for acquittal. First, the officer failed to do what was required of her when she didn't log her calibration checks. Because of this any calibration checks that may have been done cannot be considered official for ticketing purposes. Secondly, this also means that the *accuracy* of the radar was not established with sufficient evidence." If your motion is denied, you would argue these points in closing. You would also argue in closing argument that this inconsistency creates a reasonable doubt as to the accuracy of the radar, and would also focus on this being a requirement under department policy. Any other important points, for example the policy course that she hasn't taken for two years, should also be discussed in closing argument. But you must focus all of this on the *inconsistency* that you've produced, and what it means in regards to the reasonable doubt standard. In this way you also make a record for appeal purposes, if needed.

Factual Scenario #2

You want to cross-examine an officer about his competence with regards to radar and the radar he used to ticket you with. He radars you while he's sitting in his patrol vehicle under a bridge.

Q. Sir, you received radar training from the State Highway Patrol?

A. Yes, as I said earlier I went to the training academy.

Q. Where you received radar training, right?

A. Right.

Q. You went there in 1994?

A. Yes.

Q. You received instruction on different types of radars there?

A. Yes.

Q. And about how radar works?

A. Yes.

Q. This is all important to know, so you'll know how to correct for any errors or detect any problems you're having?

A. Sure.

Q. You received training on the particular radar you used in this incident?

A. Yes.

Q. I noticed the date on the certificate of training that was introduced earlier (The prosecutor may have introduced this to show he was trained). It was dated April, 1998, right?

A. Right.

Q. So you've received additional training after your academy training?

A. Yes, that's right.

Q. That training was a one-day practical application setting?

A. Well, no. It went half the week and there were classroom sessions.

Q. So you received instruction on this particular radar, its strengths and weaknesses, and how to compensate for the weaknesses?

A. Sure. I'm not sure what you mean by weaknesses though.

Q. Well, certain things that might affect the radars accuracy. These things exist, right?

A. Yes.

Q. That's because of how radar works?

A. Right.

Q. Well, basically, how does it work? (If he knows, let him explain. If he doesn't, all the better. It's based on the Doppler principle: If your car is moving away from his radar, then electromagnetic radiation shot at your car and reflected back to the radar will be stretched in proportion to the speed your going, which is then calculated. If your car is moving towards his radar, then the em-radiation is compressed in proportion to your speed, which can be calculated.)

A. Uh-uhm (or) Radar is based on the Doppler principle...

Q. And because of how it works, certain errors can occur?

A. Yes.

Q. As you said, you were taught some of these potential errors during your various training, so that you could adequately detect and cure any problems?

A. Yes.

Q. For instance, cosine error?

A. Right.

Q. What's cosine error?

A. Uh-uhm (or)

Q. And another is 'multiple reflection,' which can occur when, say, a larger vehicle is moving past yours at a slow speed, making your radar add that vehicle's speed with my vehicle?

A. Right.

Q. Actually, you were taught this is called shadowing, right?

A. Well, I'm not sure.

Q. Multiple reflection occurs when there are large stationary objects, like buildings or bridges, as in this case today, that can create multiple radar reflections back into your radar, right?

A. I think so.

Q. And these are all potential problems with your radar?

A. Yes.

Q. That's why you were given training on them?

A. Right.

Q. So you can know these potential errors exist; if you don't know or understand them, then they could occur right under your nose and you wouldn't know you were measuring the wrong speed, would you?

A. Possibly not.

You may continue crossing like this for any other questions on competency you may feel are appropriate to your case. In this way, you question the officer's competency to *use, test* or *calibrate* the radar.

These are things the prosecution must show. If it goes good for you, i.e. you ask the officer about radar and he talks about last nights MASH rerun, then you've got grounds for a motion for a judgment of acquittal, "Your honor, the prosecution failed to establish that the officer was competent to properly use the radar in question. This is something they must establish in order to support a conviction of a speeding charge based on radar." In any case, it's a good inconsistency that you should focus on in your closing argument.

Factual Scenario #3

Officer standing outside his car, glancing at his radar inside the car and waving cars down as they pass for speeding violation. Ever seen this done? You want to question on tracking history.

Q. Sir, when you saw my car you were standing outside of yours?

A. Yes.

Q. Your radar was inside your vehicle?

A. Yes, but I could see it. (Sometimes they'll have another officer with them. This may be trouble for the prosecutor, and will be if they don't also have both come to trial.)

Q. It was just outside a school district?

A. Yes.

Q. And high school had just let out about fifteen minutes before?

A. Right.

Q. So there was moderate to heavy traffic?

A. I'd say, yes.

Q. Well, that's what you marked on the ticket, right?

A. I believe so, yes.

Q. Some of those cars were passing by you?

A. Right.

Q. Others you had already waved over?

A. Yes.

Q. You were on the side of the street, right?

A. Yes.

Q. And you had to wave cars down?

A. Yes.

Q. Almost stand in front of them, like with mine, to make sure they knew you were stopping them?

A. I didn't stand in front of them, but I did have to wave them down.

Q. You were being careful?

A. Of course.

Q. You know what tracking history is, right?

A. Sure. We track the vehicles we pull over.

Q. What does tracking history include? (The answer should be visual identification, matching radar visual display, and matching radar audio monitor. See chapter 11. If he doesn't, then you should ask him about each element in particular and have him affirm its importance as part of his tracking history)

Q. Now, doing a tracking history is a significant and important part of speed enforcement, right?

A. Yes.

Q. That's because you have to make sure the car you spot is actually the car the radar spots too…what you see is what the radar sees?

A. Well, I have to make sure you're the car that's speeding.

Q. That means you must visually identify my vehicle as speeding?

A. Yes.

Q. The radar visual display must show a violation?

A. Yes.

Q. And you have to listen to the audio monitor, which must indicate that the vehicle you're tracking is the right vehicle?

A. Right.

Q. You have to do this because radar is susceptible to different types of errors, right?

A. Right.

Q. For instance, if there's moderate or heavy traffic, then what car you might visually identify as speeding and what car's speed the radar is visually showing might be different?

A. Yes.

Q. The radar might be picking up another vehicle?

A. It's possible.

Q. Likewise, if you didn't adequately hear the radar's audio monitor, then you wouldn't be able to tell if the radar was actually picking up the same car you think it is?

A. Right.

Q. The audio monitor's pitch wouldn't change like it's supposed to, right?

A. That's right.

Q. So these are the crucial elements of tracking history, right?

A. Yes.

Q. And if there are external circumstances that may impede an accurate radar reading, for instance if it's raining, then it's even more important that your tracking history be precise, isn't it?

A. Yes, but it's always important.

Q. Because you were trained that tracking history is an essential part in a traffic ticket, right?

A. Correct.

Q. Something that must be done with precision to ensure you're not ticketing an innocent person?

A. That's right.

Q. So, sir, you said you were outside your vehicle?

A. Yes.

Q. Numerous cars passing by?

A. As I said.

Q. It's fair to say a good amount of noise, those various noises that cars do make? (Produce inconsistency with audio monitor)

A. Some noise.

Q. The wheels of cars moving across the roadway?

A. Right.

Q. And the engines?

A. Yes.

Q. You were partially preoccupied with taking care not to get hurt as you waved cars down, right? (Producing inconsistency with officer's visual identification and subsequent correlation with visual and audio displays)

A. Sure, but I wasn't *preoccupied*. I was just taking care.

Q. Didn't want to interrupt the flow of traffic, did you?

A. Not if I didn't have to.

Q. You also said you had waved over other cars down just before mine? (Producing inconsistency with radars visual display indication)

A. Yes.

Q. There were other cars speeding on that roadway while you say I was too?

A. Yes.

Q. And the traffic was moderate to heavy? (Inference: radar detecting other cars)

A. Yes.

Q. Yet your radar had to be in automatic mode, because you weren't in the car to operate it, right?

A. Yes, it was in automatic mode.

Q. That means that the radar wasn't pointed at any car, like mine, *specifically*. It was pointed generally across the roadway?

A. Right.

Q. So could pick up any car's speed?

A. Yes.

In closing argument, you'll focus on all these aspects of tracking history, including how imperative it was for the officer to be very precise given the precisions. With this heightened criteria of precision, and considering how he did handle his tracking history, you've produced reasonable doubts as to the reliability of what the radar actually detected.

Once again, I emphasize that you don't need to memorize your questions. You can bring typed or written questions to court. Take your time, be professional and confident, and ask each question methodically. And *yes*, you *should* be detailed like this. There are those that advise, "In and out, that's what cross-examination is all about. You've got to get into your subject, ask a few pointed questions and then get out as quick as possible." My answer to that? One word: Bologna, and not the non-fathead kind either. More on this later.

It's really good to get the manual and all other documents I mentioned for the radar. Request discovery. Motion for discovery. Motion for production. Call and ask the police department if you can come down and look at the manual. Make copies, make notes. Just get the information.

LASER

Light Amplification by Stimulated Emission of Radiation. That's where the acronym comes from. Some people refer to lasers as **LIDAR**, which comes from **LI**ght **D**etection **A**nd **R**anging, which shows it's analogous to RADAR. The main differences between radar and laser (if you care) are that lasers are a much higher frequency and travel in much tighter beams. But it's the same stuff, electromagnetic radiation (just like light that we can see is). That's all that a radar/laser detector is, by the way—an eye that can *see* the frequencies of radar and laser. You know how you can see light from miles away? If it's dark, you can see a smoke's cherry from great distances. Imagine, if you could see in the frequencies of radar and laser, you could see them 'shining' and 'popping' from the police vehicles far, far away. Not only that, but you could *see* the electromagnetic transmission of the radio station you were listening to (as well as all the other ones you weren't). Talk about information saturation. You would *really* turn into an attentive driver then.

Anyway, the cross-examination techniques discussed above for radar are also applicable to cross-examining officers on their use of lasers. Sweep error is a good one to question on. They had better have done the scope alignment and calibration tests too. There are additional types of errors associated with the use of lasers that may be applicable to your case. Here are some examples.

1   *Prismatic error*: If the laser is directed through an angled window, the window will separate out the laser into component colors. This bends the light, and so what's reflected to the patrol vehicle is not the actual attempted target or an accurate target speed.

2   *Reflection influence*: On hot or bright days there may be a mirror image of your vehicle on the road. The laser may target the mirror image first, before reflecting off your vehicle, thereby creating a faster speed. This also can occur if the roads are very wet, or if there's a puddle of water between you and the patrol vehicle (the laser targets the puddle first, thereby creating a longer distance, and subsequent faster speed for your vehicle).

3   *Sweep error*: I mentioned this error before when discussing lasers. This occurs when the laser is not steady, or the target shifts so that the laser beam sweeps across the target. Being a narrow beam, the laser targets particular parts of your vehicle, unlike the broad beam radar that fires at your entire vehicle. This may produce a calculation of a greater distance, and hence faster speed for your vehicle. To correct for this, some lasers have built in tracking devices, but the laser operator must still be aware of the effect and hold the laser steadily. Tracking history is also important in reducing this error. It's a good one to cross-examine an officer on. *If they don't know*

what sweep error is, then they don't know how to correct for it. Who knows, then, if the laser was subject to this error in your case?

4 *Targeting:* If your vehicle is far enough away, it is possible, since the laser beam does spread out, for the officer to accidentally target another vehicle instead of yours. An officer handles this potential error by conducting a proper tracking history. Many of these various errors can be reduced by a solid tracking history; that's why tracking history is so essential, and must be adequately done to sustain a speeding conviction. This should be brought up in your motion for acquittal and your closing argument.

5 *Weather:* The laser will be adversely affected by rain, fog, sleet and such weather conditions.

There are also certain tests that must be conducted for lasers.

1 *Scope alignment test:* This is a very important test for lasers. No laser should be put in service, or used on any particular day, unless an alignment test is properly done. This tests whether the laser is aimed properly, and so if what is being targeted is actually what the laser is targeting (That's right, just because the little red dot is pointed at something, doesn't mean that's where the bullet is going to go). The laser's owner/operators manual will cover how this test should be done.

2 *Calibration test:* This test is analogous to the radar calibration tests, in that it must be done to ensure that the laser will accurately record distance and speed data. It should be done before and after the officer's shift.

Section Five

Practice

17

To begin with

This section covers the various stages of the traffic system and the part you play in each. Here, you'll apply what you've learned in the previous sections in various ways. You need to know when to do this. You need to know how. This way, you can take advantage of your work.

18

General considerations and ODP

Trial by Jury

Juveniles: no trial by jury. Adults, in some instances you may request a trial by jury. *See* Chapter 2.

What do I recommend? Well, first of all, you have to make up your own minds. But unless the most egregious factual circumstances exist, a judge or magistrate is probably the proper choice. Despite what some say, they are fair. They do have a commitment to seeing that the executive branch (law enforcement and the prosecution) does meet the standards and is playing its part. *The trouble is, in traffic court, they don't get this opportunity near enough.* I can hear them thanking me for the extra work already, if you listen to me. But they'll agree. It's true.

Many, many more of you should be demanding that law enforcement play its proper part; that it not cut corners or get lazy; that it truly act as the people's servant, and not our master. There is *one and only one way* to do this folks…Make them. If judges and magistrates were given this opportunity more often, you'd see the system working for you. You'd see articles in the paper. You'd see law enforcement on the ball more often, instead of in the coffee shop. The legislature, as your representatives, has done its part. Its crafted traffic laws that, despite a few shortcomings I'll address, created an excellent system. The Department of Transportation and other departments of the executive branch have done their part in laying down reasonable regulations to ensure the legislative system is abided by. *But the judicial branch can't get involved unless you do.* You have to raise the case, make the complaint, motion to dismiss. A judge or magistrate can't just come into work in the morning, look at some laws, devise their own fact situation, and say, "If we've got this fact situation, then the case is dismissed," then move on to *another* fact situation. That's not how it works in our country. They sit at the bench, waiting to decide on your case if you so choose to bring it. They're on *your side.* They're public servants with a solemn duty—to protect *your* rights and liberties, and not (as so many lawyers and others would have you believe) to drop a gavel on your head. Judges and magistrates like *real people.* They like justice too. If you've got a good argument, they're there to hear it, and to rule on it. Give them the chance to, would you?

Continuances

You may need to ask the court to set a different, later date for your trial. For instance, your boss requires you to be somewhere out of town, or you may have a serious family problem to deal with. There are a number of equitable reasons that may require you to change your trial date. You can do this. *See* Appendix on Forms, Request for Continuance.

Some traffic defense books advise that you get as many continuances as you can, because this increases the chances that the officer won't show. Well, I don't know about that. I'm not sure what statistical studies they're basing that conclusion on. But if I know lawyers well enough, I'd say it's pure speculation. They're fairly good at this. I don't know though—I'm just guessing. If I were an officer I would get upset with the fact that a driver kept getting continuances, and, upset because knowing what was going down (old tricks die quick), would be that more resolved to be at court when the time came. Your guess is as good as mine, but my philosophy is: attack attack attack. Don't sidestep. Besides that, if you're filing continuances for this reason only, but nominally saying otherwise, as these other defense books suggest you do, then you're...well, breaking the law. *I categorically oppose such an approach.* Not necessarily because I'm Mr. Goodie-Two-Shoes or whatever. But because it's more *efficient,* it's the better avenue of attack; you've got a higher probability of success, of *winning* (and that's half the point here) by using the law. The other half is to *make them abide by the law.* Who will watch the watcher? *Us.* I say *use the law.* It's your tool, not theirs; it's your weapon, not theirs. Don't abuse and neglect it, like they do under the guise of authority and tradition. If you do, you stoop to their level; you dull the weapon and weaken the tool.

That being said, if you're a juvenile there is one especially good reason to get a continuance. *Everyone* agrees on this: Judges, juveniles and even grudging prosecutors. It's equitable and its smart. It's occupational driving privileges, which I'll talk about next.

Occupational Driving Privileges (ODP): Juveniles

Let me first mention a legislative deficiency in this area. Here's the basic situation. Say you're 17 1/2 years old, you've received your third speeding violation, and the court has suspended your license for a year (this is a *mandatory* suspension under §4507.162(A)(1)&(3) (Driver's License Law)). You may petition to the court to grant you ODP, effective your 18th birthday, and you'll receive them if you show that the suspension "will seriously affect [your] ability to continue in employment." *See* §4507.162(C)(2). Now, that's all fine and dandy. But let's say your two weeks away from your 18th birthday, and you receive your *second* ticket. A second violation requires a suspension for ninety days. *See* 4507.162(A)(1)&(3). Some Ohio courts have ruled that you *cannot* get ODP for a second violation (for instance, the Stark County Juvenile

Courts). Parents and their sons and daughters consider this unfair—young men and women with excellent jobs or internships *losing* them because they couldn't arrange a workable traveling schedule. It's a little quirk in the statutes that needs to be clarified. What do I recommend? Call your representatives. Write them. Go see them. *Become* the representative. Tell them about this deficiency. The more of you that do…and there are a lot of you…the better your chances of getting this changed.

If you're 17, you get your third ticket as above, and you have employment you want to keep, then talk to the prosecutor about continuing your case until just before your 18th birthday (whether you plan on pleading 'true' or not). The prosecutor may ask you to plead true in exchange for continuing your case this long. You'll have to weigh the costs and benefits and the probability that you'll win the case. If you've done all the investigation written about in the previous sections, you'll know. The reason for all of this is that, okay, you'll get your license suspended, *but you'll get ODP on your 18th birthday*; the continuances allow you to keep driving to your work for the time up until the trial, since you haven't been convicted or pled true yet. So you won't lose your job. It's equitable and reasonable. More often than not this is brought up at *pre-trial* (which I'll go into just below), and the magistrate will grant a continuance of the pre-trial, vice the trial, sometimes on the agreement that you'll plead true at the *pre-trial* just before your 18th birthday (there will never be a trial).

Finally, you still may be able to plead *not true* at the later pre-trial date (This is one of the parts grudging prosecutors don't agree with). For instance, say you agreed with the prosecutor to extend your pre-trial until a week before your 18th birthday on the basis of pleading true at that pre-trial. During this delay, you buy this book and realize you've got at least, say, thirty-seven, different legitimate defenses that numerous other defense attorneys you spoke with didn't have the foggiest clue of (someone's gotta pat me on the back). Then you go to pre-trial and say, well, I learned a lot of stuff Ms. Prosecutor, and I want to plead not true because your case against me is bogus. Can you do this? Go for it. Plead your case to the magistrate, professionally, confidently and sincerely. They'll listen. Then go to trial and beat them with their own book of rules.

Arraignment

Adults

First, some courts allow, if you plan on pleading not guilty, to enter this plea at the clerk's office within four days after receiving the ticket. It's an exception. You just have to call and find out. Second, trials *may* be conducted immediately following the arraignment, but *only* upon your written consent (and the prosecuting attorney's). *See* Rules 8(A)&10(F)–TR. Otherwise, arraignment is straightforward. You'll hurry up and get there on time, and then sit there. Then you'll stand in a line. Then you'll stand in another line. They'll have you sit down again, and then maybe you'll get the opportunity to stand in another line. While you're doing all this sitting and standing, talk to other people, show them my book, tell them where they can buy a copy, and tell them they should plead not guilty. Repeat this process with as many people as possible. Then the court will ask you for your plea.

Note this though, if you have any complaints about the ticket, such as the officer didn't write the statute number down, or didn't fill out the ticket properly, or cited you under the wrong section, then before you say your plea, ask the judge to dismiss the ticket. *Don't let the prosecutor amend the ticket.* Furthermore, remember to give the prosecutor your discovery notice and/or request.

Juveniles

You shouldn't be having your trial right after your arraignment. A pre-trial will generally be scheduled. Your arraignment should go as the adult arraignments do, so read their provisions above. The only difference is your pleas are, "True" (the analog of guilty) or "Not True" (The analog of not guilty).

Pre-trial: Juveniles

Pre-trial is set to give time to deal with any issues or concerns that you may have before setting a trial date. Pre-trial is fairly informal. You'll usually go to the same place you went to your arraignment at.

You'll sit in a lobby. You'll have a scheduled time for pre-trial in front of the magistrate. Hopefully, you'll get in there on time. The prosecutor, likely a legal intern, will talk with you and pretend they're nice. Sometimes, if they're poor with their time-management skills, they'll be rushing around frantically and rushing you around and you'll be getting in to see the magistrate late; you may not then have time to talk to her (the legal intern) about your issue. You'll get in there and sit at your table. The magistrate should already be in there. The prosecutor (legal intern) will introduce the parties. You'll then set a trial date. Before setting a trial date, you have the opportunity to bring up any issues that you may have. You may talk about possible fines, the level of the charge, or any substantive or procedural issues. This is where you raise your first oral motion to dismiss. The magistrate may even dismiss your ticket on her own motion if she feels it warranted under the circumstances.

19

Special advice to juveniles II

Important Point #1: Don't tip your hand.

Throughout your case, don't go blabbing to the prosecutor (or anyone for that matter) about all the great defenses that you have. You'll have to weigh your options and see which ones you should discuss with the magistrate and which you shouldn't mention for danger of tipping the prosecutor off. For instance, if you've gone out and measured the yield sign you were ticketed at, and found it didn't comply with the OMUTCD regulations, then bring proof to the pre-trial and show the magistrate. Ask for the case to be dismissed. If it's not (and with those facts I'd be surprised if it wasn't, as long as you've got good proof), no big deal, you'll be motioning for dismissal before trial, at trial, in the middle of trial, and after trial. You'll win if your proof is good. Often, the legal intern will get nosy before you get in to see the magistrate and ask what issues or questions you have. Well, you don't have to tell her if you don't want to discuss it with her. At the same time, if it's a sure thing, and/or you think it would be beneficial to talk with the prosecutor, then go for it.

Important Point #2: Have your parents help.

As I've said before, your parents can be a great help to you in many aspects of your fight. They're a great resource. They may know certain people. They have knowledge, experience and organizational skills. Not only that, but once they get involved they'll enjoy it too. Yes, I know, I'm *crazy*.

Important Point #3: If you believe, be defiant to the end.

Don't be argumentative or hostile. *Do* calmly stick to your guns. Your views will be attacked in all things throughout life. Believe in yourself, and you won't have to *argue* your point. You can simply, rationally and coolly give your position. The only one you care who agrees is the one who will decide your fate. In a traffic court of law, it's the magistrate. Don't be caustic or condescending. *Do* be incredulous and sarcastic when appropriate (but never with the magistrate). Never pretend you're better than others (the prosecutor, officer, other witnesses or magistrate), a common human failing. Nor should you criticize. But in human relations, especially when dealing with authority…disbelief, skepticism and sarcasm are often fitting. It often creates tension, but that's how everyone learns…the sharpest sword goes through the greatest heat, the strongest diamond withstands the highest pressure.

Don't be obsequious or overly obedient. *Do* be proud and confident. Like I've always said, pride is a good thing. Throughout life people will try and bring you down. You are your only salvation. Always be confident, professional and sincere.

Don't give up. *Do* be determined to win at all costs. You must work to win your case. This all depends on you believing in it. If you have a case, and you believe in it…stick to it with resolution. Iron wills win wars.

To believe means to know. To believe in your case, you must know about it, its facts and circumstances. If, after investigating, you don't believe in your case—if you don't *know* you're going to win…then you won't...unless someone else does, and you can't count on that. To make sure you believe, make sure you know. To make sure you know, question and look for answers. We're the only ones who can.

When it's over, forget about it. *Then* it's in the past. The thing you gain from it is knowledge to use in your experiences to come. Think about it, but don't *dwell* on it. If you win, don't wallow in it. If you lose, don't sulk or be in a huff. If you break even, have a beer. Move on to your next fight before it comes to you...because it will.

Important Point #4: Don't lose sight of the forest for the trees.

What do you want to do? *Produce Inconsistencies.* That's the proper perspective. Don't get so tangled up in reading regulations or analyzing paperwork that you forget your main goal. If the argument you're developing to produce an inconsistency is too complex, not only will you mess up, no one will understand it. All you'll produce is *incongruity* (and so a conviction).

Keep it simple, stick to simple solid points. Develop them methodically, and produce inconsistencies. Focus on these points. You can't win all the arguments.

You need only win one. Develop a few, or as many as you can concretely handle. Don't go overboard. That's where your work in the previous sections will help. You'll find the most promising avenues for producing inconsistencies. Concentrate all your energies on these avenues. Yes, you may lose a little in other areas, but it doesn't matter if you win in these points.

Important Point #5: Have an exit strategy.

All great planners and thinkers have an exit strategy. How do you do it? *Find, focus, reflect, disrupt.* Most people completely neglect this part of planning and preparation, because they're so focused on the fight itself, the internal dynamics. It's a matter of focus. Having an exit strategy gives you an idea of the parameters of your case, and how far you can take the fight. Someone once said, "If at first you don't succeed, try, try again…but then give up, there's no point in making a fool out of yourself." Well said. Be defiant, but know your limits. There comes a point when your defiance is no longer aimed at your adversary, but *yourself.* To know this point is to have an excellent grasp on your case and of yourself. To begin learning how to know this point, develop exit strategies. It's a sure road to this knowledge, because it makes you think differently. You'll have to ask, "What if?" and "What then?" What if you don't get a hold of the officer's prior statements? What if the magistrate doesn't buy your pre-trial rationale; what does that mean for your case? What if the police officer answers the question in a way different from what you expected; what then? What if the prosecution has more evidence than you thought; do you have as back up a viable plea bargain you can offer to the prosecutor…a *quid pro quo* (this for that)?

You should now see why point #4 is so important. Without it you can't have an adequate exit strategy, because you'll have *too much* to deal with. Information overload; your exit strategy will be *denial.* This won't do. Points #4 & 5 are linked, and deal with this potential problem. **Find the most promising inconsistencies, *focus* your energies on these; *reflect* on the ways the prosecution can avoid them, and *disrupt* these plans.** This should be nothing new to you by now. This book's *method* incorporates all of this. *Proof* and *Procedures* finds and focuses on producing inconsistencies; *Proof* and *Practice* reflects and disrupts the prosecutor's plans.

20

Trial day

Here are a few tips for your trial day.

As I've stressed throughout this book, be calm, confident, professional and sincere. That's all you need. If you abide by this, and you've got good arguments, you'll win. If you abide by this, and your arguments are so-so, then it'll depend on the magistrate or judge. You may win or lose, but even if you lose you stand a good chance of reduction in fine and/or sentence (which is a win in and of itself). In any case, you learn, you expand your horizons.

During trial, always speak to the judge, or when you're questioning, to the witness. Don't speak or argue with or ask questions of the prosecutor. When you make an objection, make it to the judge. Don't even *look* at the prosecutor. Listen.

Always show respect for the judge. Never raise your voice. If the judge begins to speak and you happen to be speaking at the time, stop speaking and listen to what the judge has to say. Never try to talk over the judge; lawyers do this sometimes, it's discourteous, and doesn't score you points. Wait until the judge is done her question, then take your time and respond. Every now and then, when speaking with the judge, throw in a "Your honor." Don't overdue it, you should be sincere, but it's a sign of respect. When you make an objection, pause for a moment.

The judge may rule on it without you having to explain yourself. For instance, the police officer takes the stand and starts talking about what *another officer* or *another witness* (besides you) said. You stand and object, "Objection your honor, Hearsay." Now pause for a moment. With this type of objection, you won't need to explain why this is hearsay. The judge will sustain your objection (rule for you).

Other times, after you pause the judge may signal that she wants an explanation. Then you say, "Your honor, the officer is testifying as to a statement someone else made out of court, and so it's hearsay." That's an example. Don't object, and then immediately go babbling on and on. Wait a moment, and *then* start babbling.

Dress appropriately. That means dress nicely. You don't have to wear a suit or dress and all. But be presentable.

Juveniles, a parent or guardian needs to be with you at court.

21

Trial stages

Preliminary Motions

You'll be seated at your respective tables in the courtroom. If the judge/magistrate isn't already in there, she'll enter. You should rise. Usually the judge will ask the state (the prosecutor) if they have any preliminary matters or motions to address. If you aren't already, you should stand at this time, even if the prosecutor isn't standing. The judge will tell you if she wants you to be seated. After the prosecutor is done his list of motions, if any, and you've responded to them, then the judge will ask you if you have any motions to make. Here are some motions to consider.

Motion to Amend

If they haven't done so already during this whole process (and sometimes even if they have), this is where they'll try and amend the ticket. You should always object to this.

Prosecutor. The state motions to amend the ticket to include section 4511.21(A). (et cetera: here they give their rationale, which you don't particularly care about it; here's your response)

You. (Stand if you're not already. Pause, see if the judge asks you for a response first; they should; they'll look at you and say, "Response?") Your honor, I object to this amendment. First, your honor, this amendment would change the name and identity of the crime charged against me. In addition, the police officer has the duty to fill out the ticket appropriately. When the officer pulled me over, I cooperated fully and provided him with all the information he requested. He took this information to his patrol car, and had time to fill out the ticket. Your honor, the officer should not be permitted to sidestep his duty to fill out the ticket completely and accurately.

If they don't motion to amend, and they should have, then you'll have grounds for a motion for a judgment of acquittal. Say you were charged under §4511.201(reckless operation *off-road*), but they should have charged you under §4511.20 (reckless operation *on* roadway). They present evidence that proves you were driving *on* a highway. This means they just *disproved* their charge against you, i.e. that you were driving off-road. You can motion for judgment of acquittal on these grounds.

Motion for a Separation of Witnesses

The prosecution may motion to separate witnesses. You can motion for this too, and especially if the prosecutor hasn't. What does this motion mean? If, say, the prosecution has two witnesses, if you motion for a separation of witnesses this means that while one of the witnesses is testifying the other one has to leave the courtroom. That way, they can't hear each other's stories. This prevents them from changing their own to account for inconsistencies in the other. Say there are two officers. You ask for a separation of witnesses. While one officer is testifying, the other is out of the courtroom. If, for example, it's an aerial observation ticket case, and the first officer says they tested the stopwatch at 8 that morning. Then the second officer comes back into the courtroom, takes the stand, and testifies that they tested the stopwatch at 10 that morning. A glaring inconsistency that you should hammer on and which should win you the case. Likewise, for instance, a stop sign violation where one officer says he saw you stop, but then speed through (resulting in a collision), and the other officer says you didn't stop, but drove right through (resulting in a collision). You can see the importance of this motion. You should exercise your right to this. Don't worry—this motion *doesn't* apply to you, the defendant. You are allowed to stay in the courtroom the entire time and listen to everyone tell a different story—*his or her* side of the story (The number of sides to a story is equal to the number of biased witnesses). Though it does apply to other witnesses that you may have. Motion. Your honor, I motion for a separation of witnesses.

Motion to Dismiss

If the ticket was improperly filled out, for instance, they put the wrong statute number on your ticket for the offense you were charged for, then you can motion to dismiss if you so choose. Another very good reason to motion to dismiss is if the officer, or if more than one officer was involved, any of the officers is not present at trial. Lastly, motion to dismiss if you requested production of documents at trial, and the prosecutor didn't provide you with them.

Juveniles, don't motion to dismiss if the ticket doesn't have §2151.021 (jurisdiction) on it, and the prosecution didn't motion to amend. Just leave it like that, and when the prosecution rests you'll motion for a judgment of acquittal on this ground. If you mention it in your preliminary motions, then the judge might allow the state to amend it on procedural grounds.

Motion (defect in ticket). Your honor, I motion to have this ticket dismissed on the following grounds. As the ticket indicates, the state alleges that I didn't stop at a stop sign. But on the ticket the officer cited me under section 4511.15(A), which concerns a red flashing signal. This is a defect that cannot be amended without changing the name and identity of the crime I'm charged with. Therefore, it should be dismissed.

Motion (officer not present). Your honor, I motion to dismiss this case. This ticket is based on the observation of an officer in a helicopter. This officer is not here at trial today to testify, and so I motion to dismiss.

Motion (non-production). Your honor, I motion to dismiss on the following grounds. I filed a motion for the production of numerous documents at trial today. (Show judge the motion) The state hasn't produced any of these documents your honor, and so I motion to dismiss.

Motion for Continuance

If, for instance, the judge denies your motion to dismiss (non-production), then you should motion for a continuance. Or say, you requested discovery from the prosecution, and they only yesterday afternoon gave you the information you were looking for.

Motion. Your honor, I motion for a continuance for a reasonable time to allow the state to produce these documents and to allow me time to prepare an adequate defense based upon them.

Motion. Your honor, I motion for a continuance. I requested discovery from the state twenty-seven days ago. Yet they only gave me the requested information late yesterday afternoon. I request a dismissal based on these grounds, and in the alternative a continuance to allow me to prepare an adequate defense.

Opening Statements

After preliminary motions are done, you'll have a seat. Next is opening statements. The prosecution goes first. In traffic cases the prosecution often waives the opening statement. That is, they don't give one. All the opening statement does (or at least is *supposed* to do: lawyers can't help to use an opportunity to tell everyone they're right) is tell the judge (or jury) what the evidence at trial will show. Opening statements cannot be used to *argue* (as closing *argument* is used for this). They can only be used to talk about what the evidence that you're confident will be introduced during the trial will show.

Don't make an opening statement if you're pleading your case to a judge or magistrate. It will be a waste of valuable time you should be using to find inconsistencies. If you're set on making an opening statement, there are plenty of books at the library on it. If you're going before a jury (which is not the norm), then look up one of those books. After the prosecutor has waived or given his opening statement, the judge will call you to give yours. Stand and say, "Your honor, I waive opening statement."

Prosecutor's Case-in-chief

It's now time for the prosecution to call its first witness, usually the police officer who issued the ticket (often this is the only witness). Keep in mind and take note, if the ticket you received required more than one officer (say, for instance, it was an aerial observation ticket where the helo-officer radioed down to the officer in the patrol vehicle, or you were radared by one officer and pulled over by another, and one of the officers doesn't show), then you'll be motioning on hearsay when the officer starts testifying (you should've already motioned to dismiss in your preliminary motions on the ground that both officers necessary to convict you are not present at trial) about what the other officer told her. The prosecutor will start questioning the witness they called. This is called direct examination. When they're done questioning, it will be your turn to question that witness. This is called cross-examination.

When you're done cross-examining the witness, the prosecutor will get a chance to question this witness again. This is called re-direct examination. There are some objections you may want to consider while the prosecutor is conducting his direct and re-direct examinations. (Always stand before you object)

1   *Hearsay*: As I've said, if a witness starts talking about what someone else said (besides you), then you should object on hearsay grounds. For example, the officer says, "Then Officer Schmuckatelli told me…" You should object, "Objection, your honor. Hearsay." They can testify about what *you* said if they heard it, but not anyone else. There are some exceptions to this rule (as with all rules), but nothing you need concern yourself with. If you hear something like this going on, stand and object on hearsay grounds, let the prosecutor argue his side and the judge will decide if an exception applies. Often, an officer will start testifying as to what *he* said. "Then I dropped my doughnut, which is a small cake of usually leavened and sweetened dough, cooked by frying in deep fat…and told him he better start running." Although technically hearsay, this is generally allowed. Where it gets objectionable is when the officer links what he says or does to an implied statement of someone else. For example, the officer says, "Then I asked the other driver, Beatrice Pendolf, if anyone ran the stop sign. Based on what she told me I cited the defendant…" Well, that borders on objection, and you should go ahead and object. Stand and say, "Objection, your honor. The officer's testimony is bringing hearsay information into the record."

2   *Personal Knowledge*: Often the prosecutor will have the officer testify to things she knows nothing about. For example, it's often the case that the prosecutor will ask the officer if the speed (or other) sign was put up in accordance with the OMUTCD. Well, the officer *doesn't know*, unless he's also the county engineer or someone else qualified to testify to such things. So you object, "Objection your honor. Personal

knowledge and qualification. (Pause) The officer is not qualified to testify on such matters, and even if she was there is no
evidence that she has personal knowledge as to this particular
sign's requirements and if they have all been abided by." This
question is particularly interesting, though. Here's why. It's
probably a good idea to let them ask this question and let the
officer answer, "Yes," like you know they will. Why? Because
you should be pretty confident that they don't know whether
the sign is put up in accordance with the OMUTCD. This
means you can cross-examine them on it and create a beautiful inconsistency. Ask questions like:

Q. Ma'am, you testified that the sign was put up in accordance
with OMUTCD requirements, correct?

A. Yes.

Q. The height of the sign is supposed to be five feet?

A. (Who knows) Yes.

Q. It's a business district you pulled me over in, right? (On
ticket)

A. Yes.

Q. So actually, the sign is supposed to be seven feet, right?

A. (Who knows) I'm not sure.

Q. But you're sure it was done within OMUTCD qualifications?

A. Yes.

Q. Even though you don't know what those qualifications are?

A. Uh.

Q. This sign was put in by the county?

A. I guess.

Q. You don't know who put it in, but you know it was placed in accordance with the OMUTCD?

A. I'd assume.

Q. So you don't know?

A. No.

Q. And the distance the OMUTCD requires it to be from the curb is what?

A. Uh.

Q. Tell us about the traffic studies the OMUTCD requires to be done in deciding whether to put up a traffic sign.

A. Uh.

Q. An engineering and traffic investigation wasn't done for this speed sign, was it?

A. I don't know.

Q. Did you bring the engineering and traffic investigation paperwork with you here today?

A. No.

Q. Did you know the OMUTCD requires this?

A. I'm not sure.

Get the point? Just ask questions concerning the OMUTCD requirements for the sign you were ticketed under.

3 *Foundation and authenticity*: Often the prosecutor will try and offer a document (such as a certificate of accuracy of a radar device) without establishing what's called the foundation for it. The prosecutor must have someone testify who has first hand knowledge of the document (for instance, with a certificate of accuracy, the officer testifying should be the one who conducted the tests and signed the certificate). Another

example is with an E&T investigation, when the prosecutor tries to use the officer to introduce this. That's bogus, because the E&T was probably done by the county engineer. *Whoever* did it has to testify to what it is, and if it's not the original, that it's a fair and accurate copy of the original. When the prosecution says, "The state offers exhibit 1 into evidence," you stand and object, "Objection, your honor. Lack of foundation and authenticity. (Pause) Your honor, the witness cannot establish a foundation or authenticate this copy because they never saw the original, so they can't testify to it being a fair and accurate copy." Or, "Objection your honor. Lack of foundation. (Pause) Your honor, the officer wasn't the one who did the test on the radar, so can't attest to the certificate of accuracy."

4 *Leading*: During direct and re-direct, the prosecution cannot ask what are called leading questions. For example, "You saw him speeding, didn't you?" Or, "He then told you he was guilty?" Or, "You also did an external calibration, right?" Any question like this, that suggests an answer, is leading and you can object to it. "Objection, your honor. Leading." Now, don't get carried away. If the prosecutor asks something like, "You work for the Dunkin police department, right?" don't go objecting. This is a preliminary matter, something that no one disputes, and so you don't need to go aggravating people by objecting (unless you really dispute his employment). Either way, have fun with it. When the prosecution does their *cross-examination*, they are allowed to ask leading questions. All the other objections apply though.

One important note: The prosecution *cannot* introduce the ticket into evidence. If they try, object on hearsay grounds. Also, you should object if the prosecution gives the ticket to the officer and asks her to read off of it. Object before the officer starts reading from it. The officer shouldn't be allowed to testify with the ticket in her hand. After the prosecutor and you have questioned the first witness, then the next witness will take the stand. The process above will be repeated.

Your cross-examination

Just some tips for when you cross-examine. Take your time. Many lawyers say you need to be speedy with your questions, because you don't want to give the witness time to think. Dubious advice. *You* take the seat on a witness stand, with everyone watching you, and see how much 'time' you have to think. The truth is, if you ask too quickly you may confuse the fact-finder (judge or jury), and may get confused yourself. Take your time; be methodical.

You don't need to memorize your questions. You can have them written or typed, and bring them in to court like that. Just be sure to understand your questions and their purpose. That way, if something comes up you can modify them.

Many lawyers also say that during cross-examination, "you need to get in and out quickly." They say to only ask a few questions, then "snap," move on quickly to your next topic, "like a lion." No kidding, that's what they tell me. First off, lions don't hunt. Lionesses do. And they're not "in and out." They take their time, scope out the whole scene, making sure the timing is *just* right, and then, *boom*, they jump out from behind a tree and tear the ass off of some dumb, unsuspecting water buffalo. That's how you cross-examine. That's why you don't need to rush your questions, because you've framed them in such a way that the witness doesn't know where you're coming from. Furthermore, it's often the case that the whole incident is unclear. Often, the prosecutor will only ask questions pertaining to what he wants to prove, and won't sufficiently develop the entire scene. Well, quite frequently, the inconsistencies are hiding in the areas that haven't been cleared. If you take your time in cross-examination, you can lift this fog and find some inconsistencies that were previously hidden. That's why, sometimes, cross-examination can be laborious. Lawyers in the know realize this. Most lawyers don't, and are too anxious to get right to the attack before developing the testimony properly (They're like the amateur chess player who immediately attacks and gets trounced because they open up too quickly and expose their weaknesses). Clearing the terrain shuts off escape routes for the witness; otherwise he can come up with a way to get around your questioning. This is related to developing exit strategies that I told you about before. If you develop your cross-examination, you can close and lock those doors to passageways the witness would otherwise use to run. So don't rush, develop your cross-examination.

At the same time, make sure your questions have a purpose. Never ask the witness "Why?" on cross-examination. It just gives them a way to justify all the inconsistencies you've shown.

When you ask questions, use the *leading* form that I have shown you throughout the book.

Besides using the ideas you've gleaned from reading my cross-examinations throughout this book, generally you should consider things such as the witness' perception of the events, memory of them, knowledge concerning various requirements (such as radar, laser, et cetera), and prior statements.

Despite how most lawyers act, and what most lawyers think, cross-examination is not a time when you beat up on the witness, intimidate him, yell and cajole, try and make him look silly. You'll only end up doing this to yourself. Be professional, confident and calm. Be incredulous too, if the moment or witness warrants it. Your intermediate goals in cross-examination are getting information helpful to your case and testing the knowledge and credibility of the witness. Your primary goal is, as always, to *produce inconsistencies*, however so.

If the witness gives you a hard time, don't let it get to you. Keep on with your program; repeat a question if he didn't answer it the first time. Ask him to please answer your questions. Be calm, confident and professional.

Lastly, you need to know that you don't *have to* cross-examine a witness if you don't feel you can get anything from them. If they can't help your case, then say, "No questions, your honor." When you're done cross-examining say, "No further questions your honor."

After the prosecution is done with all of their witnesses, they'll rest their case. "The state (or the people) rest."

Your First Motion for Acquittal

After the prosecution rests its case, you'll stand and motion for a judgment of acquittal. The judge will usually first ask something like, "Are you ready to proceed?" Stand and say, "Your honor, before I proceed, I motion for a judgment of acquittal on the following (insert number) grounds. First…"

It's that simple. If and when you apply the previous sections, you'll know what grounds you'll be motioning on. But, *Always* motion for a judgment of acquittal, and *always* include the insufficiency of evidence ground.

Motion. Your honor, before I proceed I motion for a judgment of acquittal based on the following three grounds. First, the prosecution has introduced insufficient evidence to prove any of the elements they must prove beyond a reasonable doubt. But in particular also, your honor, they failed to introduce sufficient evidence to identify me as the person who was in the vehicle (then go into your brief explanation of this). Another ground for my motion is that the prosecution failed to establish jurisdiction. Lastly, your honor, the prosecution introduced evidence that this was an official traffic sign, but during cross-examination it became evident that the officer's testimony on this was seriously flawed.

With the insufficiency of evidence ground, you give the judge or magistrate leverage to grant a motion for a judgment of acquittal, even if you don't specify. The judge may have seen something you didn't (probably), and so knows that the prosecutor's case is a wash. Even though the judge or magistrate can motion on their own discretion, it's always important to give them this foundation too. Further, if you're convinced that you're right and the prosecutor and judge have made a mistake, then you want to preserve this on the record for *appeal*. You preserve it by motioning for a judgment of acquittal. You'll also renew this motion later. So always include anything you think you may appeal on.

Your Case-in-chief

Your case-in-chief is when you call your own witnesses to the stand and ask them questions, called direct examination.

To begin, recall that it is your constitutional right not to have to take the stand. There are important potential problems associated with taking the stand in a traffic ticket case, among them—you end up concerned about all the things *you're* going to say when you *do* take the stand (it's inevitable), and you forget about your main goal: *producing inconsistencies.* You're so worried about not producing your own, that you never get around to producing theirs. Remember, you don't have to say *anything.* They have to prove all the material elements beyond a reasonable doubt. Those that use the fear tactic that if you don't take the stand the judge or magistrate will assume you did *something* should leave the country...now. To take their view is not to trust our judges and magistrates, and to accuse them of being incapable of abiding by the constitutional requirements that you are innocent until proven guilty and that the fact that you didn't take the stand cannot be used against you. If the prosecutor, in closing argument, mentions that you didn't take the stand, tries to imply that you didn't because you are guilty, or *anything* of that nature, object immediately and motion for a 'mistrial.' Stand immediately and say, "Objection, your honor and motion for a mistrial. (Pause to see if the judge will grant it, or if he wants you to explain) Your honor, apparently the prosecutor doesn't think that I have any constitutional rights. He just mentioned that I didn't take the stand (Or He is implying that because I didn't take the stand I must be guilty). He isn't allowed to mention that I didn't take the stand or imply anything from this. I demand a mistrial."

If you do have other witnesses you want to call to the stand, for example, a passenger in your vehicle, then you may. Just say, "I call Joe Hemshuhorn (that's your friend) to the stand." He'll take the stand, and you ask him some questions to get him to tell what happened. Make sure you go over this with him beforehand.

Q. Please state your name for the record and spell it.

A. Joe Hemshuhorn, spelled…

Q. Where were you on December 11th, 2001?

A. I was a passenger in your car.

Q. At what time approximately?

A. Between 10 and 10:30.

Q. Who else was in the car?

A. You were.

Q. Where were we?

A. We were driving down Yellow-Brick road.

Q. What happened?

A. The officer there, he sped up on our bumper, flashed his lights and pulled us over.

Q. What happened next?

A. He gave you a ticket for doing 36 in a 35. (Obviously, you ask these open questions so that your friend can tell everyone what happened; they'll be waiting to hear with bated breath)

Q. Then what happened?

A. He got upset because you got cute with him.

Q. What do you mean?

A. Well, you asked him…

Objection (prosecutor): Hearsay.

Response (you): Your honor, this is showing the officer's state of mind and his subsequent course of action.

Judge: Overruled (in your favor)

Q. What were you saying?

A. I was saying you asked him if he played on a softball team, and he said yes. Then you told him you hope they lose every game.

Q. What happened next?

A. He gave you another ticket for driving without reasonable control.

There you have it, a brilliant and eloquent direct examination. Your direct examination of a witness should be simple: who are you; why are you here; what happened. When you're done questioning a witness, the prosecution will get up and ask him questions, called cross-examination. After this, you'll have another opportunity to question the witness, called re-direct. Re-direct is used to try and clear up any problems the prosecutor may have made in cross-examination. For instance, the prosecutor may have gotten your friend to say that he can't hear all too well. If you wanted you could get back up and ask something like, "Despite not being able to hear well, did you hear my conversation with the police? Often, re-direct is not necessary.

When you're done your direct examination of the witness, say to the judge, "No further questions at this time, your honor."

Another Motion for Acquittal

When you're done with your witnesses, look to the judge and say, "Your honor, I have no further witnesses, but before I rest my case may I renew my motion for a judgment of acquittal on the same grounds as before." If you have another ground you want to add, then by all means, "...on the same grounds as before, and also on two additional grounds." You should once again clarify all the grounds that you're motioning for a judgment of acquittal on. Technically, you're supposed to wait until you've rested your case to give this motion, but since you have the floor, what the heck. The judge or magistrate will direct you. Always renew your motion for a judgment of acquittal.

Closing Arguments

This is the final stage of the trial. The prosecutor goes first. Then you'll go. When you're done, the prosecutor gets another couple minutes to sum up his side again. The reason they get to go last is because they bear the burden of proof. That's why they get to go first too. *Focus on the inconsistencies you've shown.* This is how you'll show they haven't proven their case beyond a reasonable doubt. The slightest suspicion or inconsistency can mature into a reasonable doubt if you handle it properly. Your demeanor should be confident, professional and calm. You must be sincere. There's no need to yell. Now you can *argue* all the evidence and reasonable inferences from that evidence. Go for it. Argue what you feel, but always center it on the inconsistencies you've shown. After the prosecution is done babbling (don't sigh or make faces or anything like that while he's talking; just sit there and wait for your turn), wait until he has taken his seat, and stand.

"May it please the Court; the state has *not* shown my guilt beyond a reasonable doubt for the following three reasons. First, they didn't provide sufficient evidence to prove beyond a reasonable doubt that I was the one in the vehicle at the time. Second, there's a serious flaw in the officer's *use* of the radar that day, prohibiting him from establishing an adequate tracking history, which is required in order to prove my guilt beyond a reasonable doubt. And lastly, your honor, the other driver's testimony, Mr. Gumbaugh, contained numerous inconsistencies concerning what he saw and where he says I was when he passed through the intersection. His testimony is required to prove my guilt beyond a reasonable doubt, and since there are numerous reasonable doubts as to its credibility, the state has not met its burden."

That's the *introduction* to the judge or magistrate. Judges like it if you lay down the points you're going to be talking about, instead of going into an emotional tirade. Set down the reasons, just like I did above. The judge will likely write these down (or definitely mentally note them as a roadmap of where you're going), so he can follow you as you go. Not only that, but it greatly helps you maintain organization of your thoughts. Now you're ready to go into the *body* of your argument. It will consist of as many parts as you have reasons for why the state didn't prove your guilt beyond a reasonable doubt, each part covering one reason.

"Concerning the first reason, your honor, that the state didn't adequately identify me as the driver. The only witness that took the stand today and said I was the driver was the bus driver. Besides his testimony, there is no other evidence that identifies me as the driver of the vehicle at that time. But your honor, on cross-examination the bus driver clearly said that he didn't see my license plate until *after* I passed. He said he first noticed what he claims to be my car when the car was *along side of him*. There is no way then, that he could've *seen through* the front windshield to identify the driver. And we all know that when a bus is next to a car, as the car was when he first noticed it, while the car was passing him in the same direction, there is *no way* a bus driver can see into the car to the other side and see the driver…unless it's a *convertible*. At best he saw the back of someone's head as they drove away. This is hardly enough evidence to identify someone. But furthermore, your honor, the bus driver filled out a report, an official report that he must fill out when incidents such as these occur. That report was introduced at trial, and if you look at it you'll see that nowhere did he identify me, or *anyone else* for that matter, with *any* degree of accuracy, let alone accuracy beyond a reasonable doubt. All he wrote on the report was, "one person, maybe male, driving." That, your honor, isn't enough solid evidence to establish my identity with any degree of certainty, let alone certainty beyond a reasonable doubt. The officer knew this. The officer should have issued a *warning*, as the law requires, to the owner of the vehicle, and not cited *anyone*, based on such paltry evidence. They haven't satisfied their burden of proof of beyond a reasonable doubt on this point, and so I am *not guilty*.

Concerning the second reason, your honor, that the state failed to show that the police officer properly used the radar. The officer testified that he was outside his vehicle, close to traffic, waving vehicles down as they passed. He testified to there being moderate to heavy traffic on the road, with all that noise that accompanies such traffic. Wheels against the road, the engines running. All these noises. Yet an essential part of an adequate tracking history is his listening to the radars *audio* monitor, and *ensuring* that it corresponds to what he sees and what the radars visual display reads. He couldn't hear that audio monitor adequately above all that noise to be certain that it was tracking my vehicle, and that it was consistent with the radars visual display. Concerning this visual display, your honor, the officer said the radar was on *automatic* at the time. That means it *wasn't pointed at any specific target*, but only at the roadway in general. He also said that there were other cars speeding up and down this road, and heavy traffic. While he was standing outside his vehicle, not in control of his radar, the radar could've been, and in fact *had to be* arbitrarily picking up any vehicle it happened to initially arbitrarily target. Add to this, your honor, the fact that the officer was preoccupied with his safety, for he was on a busy road, waving down fast moving traffic…and the proposition that his tracking history was accurate enough to form the basis of a conviction *beyond a reasonable doubt*, becomes highly questionable. I don't question the officer's judgment or honesty in any way. Only that he is honestly mistaken. I *do* question the ability of *anyone* to adequately coordinate all three aspects of a tracking history: his visual identification, the radars visual display, and the radars audio monitor, when you have all this other stuff going on, in a way that there wouldn't be reasonable doubts as to its accuracy. That's exactly what we have here.

Concerning the third reason, your honor, that Mr. Gumbaugh's testimony didn't convincingly prove where my car was at the time he entered the intersection. If I was behind the yield sign, as his testimony *reasonably* implies, then I didn't fail to yield the right-of-way, and so am not guilty. If I was past the yield sign when he entered the intersection, then that in and of itself is *insufficient* to prove, beyond a reasonable doubt, that I failed to yield the right-of-way. And he offered no other testimony to establish I failed to yield the right-of-way. At best his testimony is inconclusive, which is not near enough to prove my guilt beyond a reasonable doubt. But his evidence isn't just inconclusive, your honor. It is also inconsistent. Mr. Gumbaugh first said he didn't see me. Then he said he actually *did* see me, but out of the "corner of his eye." He *couldn't say* whether I was stopped or moving slowly. As far his testimony concerning this point then, *it is a wash*. This is an important point your honor, because this means the state didn't provide enough evidence to show I *didn't* stop, beyond a reasonable doubt. We can then presume I stopped, since the state provided no other evidence to the contrary. That being the case, the evidence that there was an accident, and there was, *is not enough in itself* to show that I failed to yield the right-of-way. The state must produce other evidence...which they haven't done. All that they have is the testimony of Mr. Gumbaugh, who wasn't sure if he saw me or not. He says he watched me accelerate "right out in front of him." But then says he only noticed me at the last moment. His testimony simply doesn't provide enough solid, credible evidence to prove this element *beyond a reasonable doubt*. The prosecution needs more, but they have nothing."

Just go over each reason thoroughly. Argue the reasons. Collect the evidence concerning each reason. You'll know this *before* trial begins, because you figured out where the inconsistencies were going to be. Trial is just a way of *bringing them out* sufficiently enough to convince the judge of your case. Closing argument is the persuasive way of going over, emphasizing and summing up what inconsistencies you in fact brought out.

After you've given the segments of the body of your argument, it's time for the *conclusion*. Easy.

"Your honor, for these reasons, and other inconsistencies that you may have noticed, but that I haven't covered here for sake of time, the state hasn't proven my guilt on all the elements it's required to, and required to do so beyond *all* reasonable doubts. Their case against me is seriously lacking. They failed with the identity. They failed in showing the radar was properly used. And they failed, your honor, in showing that I didn't yield the right-of-way. Your honor, they were required to prove these elements beyond a reasonable doubt...they did not. Their evidence is incomplete, insufficient, and inconsistent. There are reasonable doubts throughout the state's case against me. For these reasons, your honor, I ask that you find me not guilty of all charges."

Done. It's straightforward: introduction, body, and conclusion. Closing argument is important. It's where you marshal all the evidence and relate it to what inconsistency it shows. It's where you make sense of the whole thing for the judge or jury. You organize it, as this book asks you to organize the information you get, for the judge. Once you're done speaking, simply sit back down. You are done for the day. If you've followed the method in this book, then you should be proud of yourself. You've done yourself and everyone else a great service, no matter what the outcome. You fought the power. You stood up for your rights.

Section Six

Complete Case
Example

For this case example, anything in brackets [ ] is for juveniles.

It's March 17th. You're driving down a road. You're friend [mother/guardian] is riding with you. Everyone has a seat belt on. For sake of the example, the road is called Lee Road. A police officer pulls you over. He asks, "Did you know you were speeding, sir?" "No," you respond. "I clocked you going 49mph. This is a 35mph zone. Is that about the speed you were going?" You respond, "I believe I was going the speed limit, officer." He asks, "Why weren't you wearing your seat belt?"" I was; I took it off after I stopped to get my wallet out of my back pocket," you tell him. You give him all the necessary information, he goes back to his police car, and returns after a few minutes. He gives you a ticket for doing 49mph in a 35mph.

You begin.

The statute number written on your ticket is 4511.21(C). [The officer didn't write 2151.021 on your ticket.] The box 'Over limits,' under the Speed is marked. The Radar box is checked. The Stationary box is also checked. The conditions on the ticket are marked as follows: Pavement dry, Visibility clear, Weather no adverse, Traffic light, Area residential, Crash No, Remarks (left blank).

Lee Road is in Powell Township, Stanley County. You go back to Lee Road where you were pulled over. This portion of the road is a straight-away. The speed limit on Lee Road is posted as 35mph in three separate places. Call the first place it was posted, traveling in your direction, Point A. (Get ready to make a diagram) There's a sidewalk going past the speed sign and continuing on in the direction you were traveling. *Before* point A, the speed limit is 55mph. After the third speed limit sign in the direction you were traveling is a speed limit sign reading 45mph. Call this Point B. In this speed zone of 35mph (between the first 35mph speed sign and the 45mph speed sign, points A and B respectively), a major road intersects Lee Road. Call it Barner Road. The closest speed limit sign posted on Lee Road after this intersection is 75 yards away. You do an accurate measuring, with the help of a friend [parent/guardian], of the speed limit signs.

The first speed sign is on ground sloped downward. It is 6 feet from the ground (measured from the bottom of the sign to the level of the top of the curb and further). The second sign, the last you passed before being pulled over, is also on sloped ground. Its height is 6 feet, 6 inches from the top level of the curb to the bottom of the sign, though it is 7 feet 2 inches to the *ground*. The third is 7 feet 5 inches in height. The 45mph speed limit sign is also 7 feet 5 inches in height. You also measure the dimensions of the signs and note their borders and lettering. You further measure their lateral clearances from the road. The first two are approximately six feet from the road. The third is three feet from the road. You take pictures of the complete signs and its surrounding road, with your friend standing beside each sign for height purposes and using a measuring device. (Note: check both directions of travel for these requirements, not just the direction you were traveling. A speed zone is unenforceable everywhere if it is unenforceable anywhere). You also take a picture of the roadway in both directions along the area you were pulled over, and finally of the intersection of Lee and Barner

Roads, along with a picture showing the distance to the first speed sign 75 yards away after this intersection.

Your arraignment is in seven days. You've been reading this book, so you've got some good ideas on what to do. You've made a checklist of what they have to show. You've made a checklist of the procedures they must follow. You've made a checklist of your most promising areas for producing inconsistencies. You've done some good research already, and know you've already got some grounds to file a Motion to Dismiss. But you want to see if you can get some more ammunition. You call up the Powell Township engineer and find out their hours of operation and where they're located. You take a drive down there and talk to the secretary, who gets the township engineer for you. You speak and he looks for the E&T investigation. He can't find one in the office, but says he'll check with the county engineer and see if they've got one on file. You thank him and give him your name and number, get his business card. He tells you he'll call back as soon as he gets some word.

Your arraignment is a day away. You've got a good feel how you're going to handle the case. You also know the document you'll give the prosecutor at arraignment: A Discovery Request. On the Discovery Request, you'll include the traditional request, plus a request for the E&T investigation, the associated Powell Township resolution or DOT request for a speed limit change, and any DOT acceptance, as well as the radar's owner/operators manual, and the officer's radar calibration and traffic logbooks. You've made a list of the other documents you'll use.

1   Motion to Dismiss (OMUTCD, E&T)
2   Request for Production (Officer's books/manuals, E&T documents)

You go to the arraignment with your ticket and Discovery Request. It's your turn to plead. You say to the judge [magistrate], "Your honor, before I enter my plea, I motion to dismiss this charge based on a defect in the ticket. This is a garden-variety speeding ticket your honor, but the police officer failed to write the appropriate sections on the ticket. He should have written section 4511.21(A) on the ticket. He didn't." The judge takes a look at your ticket. "Well, this isn't a jurisdiction that requires section 4511.21(A) to be written on the ticket, so I'll deny your motion. Are you prepared to plead?" Yes, your honor. But first may I give the prosecutor a Discovery Request and have this noted on the record, your honor?" This is done. "What is your plea?" "I plead not guilty [not true]." The judge fills out your paperwork, and gives you a copy. You ask where the clerk of courts is, and the judge tells you. You see that your trial [pre-trial] date is set for 30 days away.

It's been a few days, and you aren't sure if the prosecutor is going to respond to your request for discovery. You decide to do a Motion for Discovery for all the things you requested discovery on, and file it with the clerk of courts (duly certified that a Discovery Request was made and not responded to) as soon as you can, and send a copy to the prosecutor. Meanwhile, you called and spoke with the township engineer. He's found the documents. You go down to his office and get a copy of the E&T investigation and the other applicable documents.

You also file a Motion for a Request for Production of these same documents, including the officer's logbooks, and also documents showing the signs were properly illuminated or reflectorized (because you want the prosecutor to do a little work for his pay) with the clerk of courts, and send a copy to the prosecutor.

You study the E&T investigation, and see that a private firm has done the investigation, and not the township or county engineer. You also note that no terminal points are mentioned in the E&T, Township resolution or DOT acceptance. The E&T investigation does establish the area as a residential one. You're now ready to do and file a Motion to Dismiss. What arguments will you address?

a. *OMUTCD heights.* You write something like: The Ohio Manual of Uniform Traffic Control Devices (OMUTCD) requires that signs in residential areas where pedestrian traffic is likely to occur must be at least 7 feet in height. *See* OMUTCD, §2E–4(Rev. 20). The signs were located in a residential area. The pictures included with this motion clearly show sidewalks, and so pedestrian traffic was likely. The picture labeled number one shows the first sign designating this speed zone of 35mph. It is only 6 feet in height, and so doesn't meet the OMUTCD requirements. Included herein is an affidavit of the person shown in the pictures, John Mulkenberry, attesting to the measurements and their correctness. The speed zone here is thus not enforceable. The picture labeled number 2 shows the second sign, which is posted approximately 100 yards from were I was pulled over. Its height is only 6 feet 6 inches. This doesn't meet the OMUTCD requirements. As such, the purported speed zone is unenforceable, since these are unofficial traffic signs. *See* §§4511.11(A)&(D), 4511.12¶¶1&2. The true speed limit is the prima facie 55mph. *See* §4511.21(B)(5). As I was ticketed as going 49mph, I was in violation of no law, and my ticket must be dismissed.

b. *OMUTCD lateral clearances.*

The OMUTCD requires traffic signs have at least a 12-foot lateral clearance from the roadway. *See* OMUTCD, §2E–5(Rev. 20). As picture number 3 shows, the third speed limit sign in this speed zone was only 3 feet from the roadway. As pictures numbers 1 and 2 show, these signs are approximately 6 feet from the roadway, and so none of them are in accordance with the OMUTCD requirement of a 12-foot lateral clearance. Therefore, this speed zone isn't in keeping with the OMUTCD requirements, containing unofficial traffic control devices, and as such is unenforceable under law. *See* §§4511.11(A)&(D), 4511.12¶¶1&2. The prima facie speed limit of 55mph controls, and since I was traveling at 49mph, my ticket must be dismissed.

c. *Terminal Points*. The OMUTCD requires a speed limit sign be posted at the beginning terminal point of a speed zone stating what the speed limit is, and a speed limit sign be posted at the end of the speed limit zone stating what the new speed limit is beyond the speed zone. *See* OMUTCD, §5D–10(Rev. 20). The terminal point marking the beginning of a speed zone traveling in one direction on the roadway simultaneously functions as the terminal point marking the end of this speed zone if traveling from the opposite direction. These OMUTCD requirements are required for both directions of the purported speed zone. The OMUTCD further recommends that the terminal points be documented in the engineering and traffic investigation. *See* OMUTCD, §5D–7(Rev. 20). Nevertheless, they must be publicly documented somewhere to allow the public to review. The terminal points are not mentioned in the engineering and traffic investigation, attached to this motion. Nor are the terminal points mentioned in the Powell Township resolution or and Department of Transportation documentation. There is no proof that they were ever even established. There is then no way to determine the bounds of the alleged altered speed zone, where it begins and where it ends. It further is impossible to determine if the applicable speed signs are posted at these terminal points, if they exist at all, which no accessible public documents show. For these reasons, the 35mph speed zone is unenforceable, and my ticket must be dismissed.

d. *E&T Private Firm*. The Ohio Attorney General has specifically said that a township board of trustees may *not* contract to have a private engineering firm conduct an engineering and traffic investigation, instead of having the county or township engineer conduct it. *See* OAG 89–011. It is clear from reviewing the engineering and traffic investigation paperwork provided with this motion that the investigation was in fact done by a private engineering firm. That being the case, the 35mph speed zone is invalid and unofficial, and as such is unenforceable. My ticket must be dismissed.

e. *Major public roadway or major access point.* The OMUTCD provides that a speed zone *cannot be enforced* until standard signs have been properly installed along the roadway. *See* OMUTCD, §5D–10. This includes the posting of signs *just beyond each point* where traffic enters the street or highway from other major public roadways or major access points. *See* OMUTCD, §5D–10. The road I was ticketed on is Lee Road. Barner Road, a major access public roadway, shown in photograph 4, intersects Lee Road in the purported 35mph speed zone. Picture number 5 shows the first speed sign after this intersection, along with its distance from the intersection, which is 75 yards. This doesn't meet the OMUTCD requirements that speed signs be posted *just beyond* such intersections. As the photograph shows, there were no physical obstacles to posting the speed limit signs closer to the intersection of Lee and Barner Roads. Further, pictures 6 through 9 show various nearby intersections (labeled appropriately), along with where the speed limit signs are posted. As the pictures show, the speed signs at these intersections are all posted properly, *just beyond* the intersection. As such, this speed zone is unenforceable under law, and my ticket must be dismissed.

Make sure and include copies of all the appropriate documents when you file the Motion to Dismiss with the clerk of courts. You also include the photographs, labeled properly so the judge can refer to them. Your motion to dismiss is miraculously denied. [Your pre-trial date comes but you haven't received any discovery from the prosecutor. At the pre-trial, you motion for dismissal based on all the grounds you cited in your written motion. You also include as a ground the fact that the prosecutor hasn't abided by the Motion for Discovery. All denied. You continue with your plea of not true, and request a trial date]. If you received discovery, you went over the documents thoroughly. [You went over all prior statements too]. You note any discrepancies and make copies of all the documents you're permitted to. If you didn't receive discovery, then you'll add this to your grounds for your motion to dismiss in your preliminary motions at trial.

While inspecting the police officer's calibration log (You should have seen this during discovery, but if not the prosecutor should produce it, as you requested, at trial), you notice that the officer didn't log that he had done calibration checks before or after his shift.

You update your Producing Inconsistencies checklist, noting the strongest arguments for your trial. First, you'll argue that you were driving reasonably under the circumstances, under §4511.21(A)–TL, and so cannot be convicted. Next, you'll argue that since the officer failed to log his alleged calibrations, the state has offered insufficient and incomplete evidence to prove the radar was calibrated properly and so there is reasonable doubt as to its accuracy on the day of the incident.

Your trial day arrives. The prosecution didn't produce documents showing that the traffic signs were properly reflectorized or illuminated (OMUTCD §§2D–1, 2D–2). You'll also include this as a ground in your motion to dismiss. The prosecutor asks if you would like to change your plea. You ask him if he'd like to change his. He gives you everything you requested for production of, except the above noted documents. You review them and note to yourself that the officer failed to document any calibrations.

Judge enters courtroom. You stand. Judge takes her seat. You sit.

Preliminary Motions

Judge/Magistrate (J) (To the prosecutor): Do you have any preliminary motions?

Prosecutor (P): Yes, your honor. The state motions to amend the traffic citation to include section 4511.21(A).

J (To you): Any objections?

You (Y): Yes, your honor. This amendment would change the name and identity of the crime charged against me. Section 4511.21(A) covers a separate and distinct charge from section 4511.21(C), which I was charged under. And so pursuant to Rule 7(D) of the rules of criminal procedure, this amendment is not permitted.

J: Motion denied (Sides in your favor; the ticket cannot be amended) (To the state): Anything further?

P: No, your honor.

J (To you): Do you have any preliminary motions?

Y: Yes, your honor, I first would like to motion for a separation of witnesses. (Do this if there is more than one witness for the prosecution)

J: Granted. Any other?

Y: Yes, your honor, I motion for a dismissal of this case with prejudice for numerous reasons. Your honor, would you rather I cover one reason and then you rule on it, or would you rather I go over all of my reasons before you rule?

J: Go over all of them and then I'll rule.

Y: First, there's a defect in the ticket. The officer didn't include section 4511.21(A), as he is required to do. Second, I requested and motioned for discovery from the prosecutor. I also requested production at trial today of documents showing the speed signs in question were properly reflectorized or illuminated. The prosecution hasn't produced any such documents, though he has had ample time to, and so I motion to dismiss on this ground. Next (now go over each of the reasons you used in your *written* motion for a dismissal). [Remember, don't bring up the failure of anyone to notice §2151.021's absence on the ticket.]

J: (She'll go over each of your motions, and either grant or deny on each. If you win one, you win.)

Motions denied.

You sit down.

J (To the prosecutor): Are you ready to proceed with opening?

Prosecution waives opening.

Judge (To you): Would you like to make an opening statement?

Y: I waive opening statement, your honor.

Prosecution's Case-in-chief. They call the officer and he testifies. You make sure they cover every material element on your Proof checklist, for both the speeding offense and the requirements for radar. If not, you mark them and will use them as additional specific grounds in your motion for a judgment of acquittal. Assume they forget to cover identity and the audio monitor testimony for radar tracking.

You cross-examine

You focus your cross-examination on showing that you were driving reasonably, and that the officer didn't record his calibrations. *See* Chapter 16, Speeding and RADAR sections, respectively, for further cross-examination examples on these two topics.

Q. Good morning, sir.

A. Good morning.

Q. I'd like to ask you a few questions about this traffic citation.

A. Okay.

Q. You ticketed me for going 49 in a 35, correct?

A. That's right.

Q. You marked the 'over limits' box in my speeding ticket, didn't you?

A. I believe so.

Q. You marked the 'radar' box?

A. Yes, it's on the ticket.

Q. You marked that the pavement was dry?

A. Yes.

Q. That there was no adverse weather?

A. Right.

Q. Visibility clear?

A. Yes. It's all on the ticket.

Q. You marked that the traffic was light at the time?

A. I think I did.

Q. Your honor, I have the ticket here. (Show the prosecutor) May I approach the witness?

J: You may.

Q. Sir, this is the ticket you cited me with. (Show him the ticket) Do you see the box labeled 'Traffic?'

A. I do.

Q. It's marked 'light,' correct?

A. Yes, it is.

Q. (Keep the ticket and go back to where you were standing) You also marked that it was a residential area?

A. Yes.

Q. Finally, you marked that there was no crash?

A. Yes.

Q. In fact, there wasn't even almost a crash, right?

A. That's right?

Q. As you testified earlier, the road you pulled me over on is a straightaway?

A. Yes.

Q. By the way, you didn't mark the 'Unsafe for conditions' box on my ticket, did you?

A. No, I didn't.

Q. That's because, considering all the conditions we just went over, I wasn't driving unsafely for the conditions, was I?

A. No, you weren't.

Q. In fact, you could say I was driving reasonably under the circumstances, couldn't you?

P: Objection, your honor. This is a conclusion for the court to make and not the witness.

Y: Your honor, the officer is trained to make such observations.

J: Sustained.

Q. I was driving safely for the conditions, right?

P: Objection.

Y: Your honor, this is how the officer marked the ticket.

J: Overruled.

A. Yes, I suppose so. You weren't driving unsafely.

Q. But you ticketed me nonetheless?

A. Yes, you were going over the speed limit.

Q. Your radar indicated 49?

A. That's right.

Q. And you were confident that it read 49, because you testified that you calibrated it?

A. Yes.

Q. Now, when you calibrate your radar, you log this in your calibration logbook, right?

A. That's right.

Q. Because you're required to do so?

A. Yes.

Q. It's your department's mandatory policy?

A. Yes.

Q. As well as the law?

A. I believe so. Yes.

Q. So it's fair to say that if you didn't log a calibration in your logbook, we could assume you didn't do the required calibrations?

A. Well, unless I told you otherwise.

Q. What if you didn't write the speed you say I was going, 49, or the speed zone, 35, on the ticket, could we just take your word for it that those were the numbers?

A. No, but I did the calibrations.

Q. But sir, you didn't log them, did you?

A. (If he knows you're going to impeach him, he'll admit it. Let's say he doesn't) Yes, I did.

Q. Your honor, I have what is marked as exhibit 1 (The logbook. Show the prosecutor) May I approach the witness?

J: You may.

Q. This is your calibration logbook? (Show the logbook to the officer)

A. Yes, it is.

Q. This page here is marked March 17th? (The day of your ticket. Show the page)

A. Yes, it is.

Q. These are then all the entries you made in your logbook on that day?

A. Yes

Q. The day you ticketed me?

A. Yes.

Q. Please show the court where you logged doing the calibrations. (Hand logbook to him)

A. (Spends time looking) I can't find any entries. But I did do them.

Q. (Get logbook back, and walk back to where you were standing) You spent some time looking a moment ago, but you couldn't find any evidence of having logged these calibrations?

A. No.

Q. No log of having done calibrations before you began your shift?

A. As I said, no.

Q. No log of doing either internal or external calibrations, right?

A. That's right.

Q. No log of having done calibrations after your shift ended?

A. No.

Q. Of either internal or external calibrations?

A. Like I said, no.

Q. But these log entries are *all* required, correct?

A. Yes, they are.

Q. Thank you, sir.

Take your seat.

Prosecution doesn't re-direct.

Prosecution closes, "Your honor, the state rests."

Your Motion for a Judgment of Acquittal

J (To you): Are you ready to proceed?

Y: Your honor, I motion for a judgment of acquittal based on numerous grounds. [First, the prosecution failed to establish jurisdiction since they didn't include section 2151.021 on the ticket.] Second, the prosecution offered no evidence to establish identity. Also, the state lacks sufficient evidence to prove my guilt beyond a reasonable doubt for any of the elements they are required to prove. Further, the state was required to produce evidence as to the functioning of the radars audio monitor. This is a required part of the officer's tracking history, to ensure that the car he's watching is the same car the radar is 'watching.' They offered no evidence of this essential part of the officer's tracking history. Next, your honor, the state failed to introduce sufficient evidence to show that the radar was adequately calibrated, and so that it was functioning properly. The officer is required by department policy and law to log all his calibration checks. He didn't log any of them. Lastly, your honor, the officer admitted that I was driving safely for the conditions. That's why he didn't cite me under section 4511.21(A). But, your honor, even if I was going 49mph, if I was driving reasonably under the circumstances, then

I cannot be convicted of the charge. The officer's testimony, the ticket, and all the conditions at the time of the incident, weather, road, traffic…all of them, show that I was, in fact driving reasonably under the circumstances. The state has offered no evidence to rebut this proof. For these reasons, and for all the reasons I mentioned in my motion for dismissal, I request a motion for a judgment of acquittal. (*Note*: Don't forget, you don't have to memorize any of your questions or statements {like some books tell you}. Write it or type it out and use this at the trial.)

J: (If he's an utter loon, he'll deny) Motion denied.

P: Wow, thanks your honor.

You sit down.

Your Case-in-chief

You call your friend [mother] to the stand, who was a passenger in your car the day you were cited. She testifies to your driving, the weather conditions, and all prevailing conditions at the time that show you were driving reasonably under the circumstances. Here are the basic steps how:

J (To you): Are you ready to proceed with your case-in-chief?

Y: Yes, your honor.

J: Call your first witness.

Y: The defense calls Mrs. Holly Hollumperlaxer to the stand.

Q. Please state your name for the record and spell it.

Y. My name is Mrs. Holly Hollumperlaxer, last name spelled…

Q. What is your relation to me?

A. I'm your mother.

Q. Where were you on March 17, 2001?

A. My child is innocent! That officer is a mean man!

P: Objection!

J: Ma'am, *please* just answer the question.

Y: Mom, please…control yourself.

A. I was with you in your car when *he* pulled us over.

Q. What were the weather conditions?

A. Beautiful. You were driving reasonably.

Q. And the road and traffic conditions?

A. Beautiful. You were driving reasonably.

Q. Did you have your seat belt on?

A. Yes, and so did you. You were driving reasonably.

P: Your honor!

Your mom: What?! What did I do?

Et cetera.

Prosecution cross-examines, if they dare.

You don't re-direct. Thank the Lord.

Your Renewed Motion for a Judgment of Acquittal. Before you rest your case, you ask the judge if you may renew your motion for acquittal.

> Y: Your honor, before I rest my case I would like to renew my motion for a judgment of acquittal.
>
> J: Well, we usually do that after both parties have rested.
>
> Y: The defense rests.
>
> J: Any other motions from either party?

Y: Your honor, I would like to renew my motion for a judgment of acquittal.

J: Very well.

Y: Your honor, I renew my motion for a judgment of acquittal on the same grounds I initially motioned for a judgment of acquittal. (Now include any other grounds that you may have forgotten before, or that you may have thought of).

J: Motion denied. Is the state ready to give its closing argument?

Prosecution gives closing argument.

You give your closing argument, an eloquent soliloquy of justice and injustice, liberty, freedom and what not. You keep it simple though, sticking to the format provided for you in this book. You focus on the inconsistencies in the case, and on the subjects you've drawn out in cross-examination. You may include language identical to the language you used in your motions for acquittal. First, you talk about the police officer not logging his calibrations properly. You next talk about the absence of any evidence concerning the audio monitor, and failure to establish identity. Then you talk about the fact that you were driving reasonably under the circumstances, and there is no evidence to the contrary of that. Then, if you wish, you can go over all the other problems you've been noting, from the failure of the prosecutor to produce all requested documents at trial, to improperly posted speed limit signs.

Prosecution gives rebuttal.

The Judge/Magistrate now ponders at her perch. After scratching around and filling out some paperwork, she pauses, looks up, and then proclaims that: "For the reasons that the state has failed to provide sufficient evidence to prove beyond a reasonable doubt that the radar was properly tested and used on the day of the incident, and for the state's failure to rebut the substantial evidence provided that the driver was, in fact, driving reasonably under the prevailing conditions and so in accordance with the law…the defendant is found *not guilty*, and is hereby acquitted of all charges…You are free to go."

Make sure and get any money they required you to post for trial. They'll tell you they'll mail it to you. Bank interest continuously accrues, even for wayward governments. Request you receive a check right then. Most importantly though,

You're free to *go!*

Appendix

Helpful Contacts

Websites

www.motorists.org (Home website of the National Motorists Association)

www.motorists.com/oh (Home website of the Ohio Chapter of the National Motorists Association)

www.newromesucks.com (Home website of the 'resistance' movement against New Rome traffic enforcement policy)

www.findlaw.com (Website for searching statutes and case law)

www.onlinedocs.andersonpublishing.com (Ohio statutes)

www.ci.north-olmsted.oh.us/FUNCTIONS/DEPARTMENTS/Engineering/OMUTCD.htm (About the Ohio Manual of Uniform Traffic Control Devices)

www.dot.state.oh.us (Ohio Department of Transportation)

Libraries

Organized by City

Ada

Ohio Northern University
Taggart Law Library
(419) 772-1875

Akron

Akron Law Library Association
2209 South High Street, 4th Floor
(330) 643-2804

Brouse McDowell
106 S.Main Street
(330) 535-5711

SRM Library Services
3000 Silver Maple Drive
(330) 666-5156

University of Akron Law Library
(330) 972-7330

Athens

Athens County Law Library Association
Athens County Courthouse, 4th Floor
(740) 593-8893

Batavia

Clermont County Law Library Association
270 Main Street
(513) 732-7109

Bellefontaine

Logan County Law Library Association
101 S.Main Street, Room 19
(937) 592-5846

Bowling Green

Wood County Law Library
168 South Main Street
(419) 353-3921

Bucyrus

Crawford County Law Library
117 N. Sandusky Avenue
(419) 562-7863

Cambridge

Guernsey County Law Library
Guernsey County Courthouse
(740) 432-9258

Canton

Stark County Law Library Association
110 Central Plaza South, Suite 401
(330) 451-7380

Chardon
Geauga County Law Library Association
100 Short Court Street, Suite BA
(440) 285-2222

Chillicothe
Ross County Law Library
28 North Paint Street Basement
(740) 773-1075

Cincinnati
Cincinnati Law Library Association
601 Hamilton County Courthouse
1000 Main Street
(513) 946-5300

Sixth Circuit Library for the U.S. Courts
317 Potter Stewart U.S. Courthouse
(513) 564-7321

University of Cincinnati College of Law
Robert S. Marx Law Library
(513) 556-0163

Circleville
Pickaway County Law Library Association
(614) 474-6026

Cleveland
Case Western Reserve University
School of Law Library

11075 East Blvd.
(216) 368-2792

Cleveland Law Library Association
404 Cuyahoga County Courthouse
1 Lakeside Avenue
(216) 861-5070

Cleveland State University
Cleveland-Marshall College of Law Library
1801 Euclid Avenue
(216) 687-3547

Legal Aid Society of Cleveland
1223 West 6th Street
(216) 687-1900

U.S. Courts Library
319 U.S. Courthouse
(216) 522-2253

Columbus

Capital University Law Library
303 East Broad Street
(614) 236-6464

Columbus Law Library Association
369 South High Street, 10th Floor
(614) 221-4181

Office of the Ohio Public Defender
8 E. Long Street, 11th Floor
(614) 466-5394

Ohio Attorney General Library
30 E. Broad Street, 15th Floor
(614) 466-4534

Ohio State University Moritz Law Library
55 W. 12th Avenue
(614) 292-6691

Supreme Court of Ohio Law Library
30 E. Broad Street, 4th Floor
(614) 466-2044

Coshocton
Coshocton County Law Library
305 Main Street
(740) 622-6464

Dayton
Dayton Law Library Association
41 North Perry Street
(937) 225-4496

University of Dayton Zimmerman Law Library
300 College Park
(937) 229-2314

Defiance

Defiance County Law Library Association
510 Court Street
(419) 782-1186

Elyria

Lorain County Law Library Association
226 Middle Avenue
(440) 329-5567

Findlay

Hancock County Law Library Association
300 S.Main Street
(419) 424-7077

Fostoria

Seneca County Law Library
110 E. North Street
(419) 435-5544

Fremont

Sandusky County Law Library Courthouse
100 N. Park Avenue
(419) 334-6165

Gallipolis

Gallia County Law Library Association
18 Locust Street, Room 1260
(740) 446-7478

Georgetown
Brown County Law Library
204D Cherry Street
(937) 378-3101

Greenville
Greenville Law Library Association
124 W. 5th Street
(937) 547-9741

Hamilton
Butler County Law Library Association
10 Journal Square, Suite 200
(513) 887-3696

Hillsboro
Highland County Law Library Association
High and Main Streets
(937) 393-4863

Ironton
Lawrence County Law Library
4th Floor Annex Courthouse
(740) 533-0582

Jefferson
Ashtabula County Law Library Association
25 W. Jefferson Street
(216) 576-8002

Lancaster

Fairfield County Law Library
224 E. Main Street, Rm. 102
(740) 687-7116

Lebanon

Warren County Law Library Association
500 Justice Drive
(513) 695-1381

Lima

Allen County Law Library Association
3233 Spencerville Road
(419) 999-4272

Lisbon

Columbiana County Law Library
105 S. Market Street
(330) 420-3662

London

Madison County Law Library
1 N. Main Street, Room 205
(740) 852-9515

Mansfield

Richland County Law Library Association
50 Park Avenue East
(419) 774-5595

Marietta
Washington County Law Library
205 Putnam Street
(740) 373-6623

Marysville
Union County Law Library
215 West Fifth Street
(937) 645-3000

Marion
Marion County Law Library Association
100 N.Main Street
(740) 383-3509

Medina
Medina County Law Library
93 Public Square
(330) 725-9744

Medina County Law Library (branch)
225 E. Liberty
(330) 723-5450

Mount Gilead
Morrow County Law Library Association
48 E. High Street
(419) 946-6578

New Philadelphia
Tuscarawas County Law Library
101 E. High Avenue
(330) 364-3703

Newark
Licking County Law Library Association
65 E.Main Street, Lower Level
(740) 349-6561

Painesville
Lake County Law Library Association
47 N. Park Place
(440) 350-2899

Paulding
Paulding County Law Library Association
200 N.Williams Street
(419) 399-2217

Ravenna
Portage County Law Library
241 South Chestnut Street
(330) 297-3661

Sandusky
Wyandot County Law Library
109 S. Sandusky Avenue, Room 15
(419) 294-4088

Springfield

Clark County Law Library Association
101 N. Limestone Street
(937) 328-2477

Steubenville

Jefferson County Law Library Association
County Court House, 3rd Floor
(740) 283-8553

Tiffin

Seneca County Law Library
Courthouse, 4th Floor
103 S.Washington Street
(419) 447-7422

Toledo

Toledo Law Association
905 Jackson Street
(419) 213-4747

U.S. Courts Library
418 U.S. Courthouse
1716 Speilbusch
(419) 259-7539

University of Toledo College of Law Library
2801 W. Bancroft Street
(419) 530-2821

Troy

Miami County Law Library Association
201 W.Main Street
(937) 332-6861

Urbana

Champaign County Law Library
200 N.Main Street
(937) 653-2709

Wapakoneta

Auglaize County Law Library
201 Willipie Street, Suite 207
(419) 738-4713

Warren

Trumbull County Law Library Association
120 High Street, N.W.
(330) 675-2525

Washington Court House

Fayette County Law Library Association
Fayette County Courthouse Building, Ground Floor
(740) 335-3608

Wilmington

Clinton County Law Library Association
46 S. South Street
(937) 382-2428

Xenia

Greene County Law Library Association
Green County Courthouse, Room 309
(937) 376-5115

Youngstown

Mahoning Law Library Association
Courthouse, 4th Floor
120 Market Street
(330) 740-2295

Forms and Checklists

Here is a compilation of some important checklists and general forms. When needed, brackets, [ ], are used to signify an entry for juveniles. Similar and more numerous forms can be found at your local library (reference section). The forms below are general examples, and aren't meant as direction as to what to motion for or request. Further, it is not perfectly clear as to what specific documents are required to be turned over to you, and for that matter what any given office will in fact turn over. Generally, motions or requests are filed with the appropriate clerk or courts and/or the prosecutor's office. You should contact the clerk of courts or prosecutor to find out where you need to file your requests or motions. The checklists aren't intended to be complete categorizations, but only to give you an idea of how to structure your own.

(1) Request for trial by jury

(2) Proof checklist

(3) Procedures checklist

(4) Producing Inconsistencies checklist

(5) Notice Request

(6) Discovery Request

(7) Discovery Request (E&T)

(8) Discovery Request (Speeding)

(9) Motion for Discovery (general, E&T, Speeding)

(10) Motion for Production (E&T, Signs, Studies, various)

(11) Motion to Dismiss (Defect in ticket, E&T, Signs, et cetera)

(12) Request for Continuance

Request for trial by jury

IN THE COURT OF COMMON PLEAS
X COUNTY, OHIO

IN THE MATTER OF:	:	CASE NO. CT 02-111
JOHN H. DOE:	:	JUDGE SCHMUCKATELLI
D/O/B: 8-27-67		
Alleged Traffic Offender:	:	**REQUEST FOR TRIAL BY JURY**

Pursuant to Rule 9(A) of the Ohio Traffic Rules, and Rule 23(A) of the Ohio Rules of Criminal Procedure, I, John H. Doe, the Defendant, hereby demand a jury trial for the above-captioned case.

_____

John H. Doe
0000 Yuckalittle Drive
Ohio

Proof Checklist

Elements   *Evidence*
1. Identity   Witnesses testimony
2. Venue   Officer's testimony
3. [Age]
4. [Traffic Jurisdiction: 2151.021]
5. Uniform
6. Vehicle
7. Specific elements of charge

Procedures Checklist

Traffic Sign	*Regulation potentially violated*
1. Height	7 ft required, but only 5 ft 11 in
2. Lateral clearance	
3. Location	
4. Dimensions	
5. Lettering	
6. Borders	
7. Reflectorization/Illumination	

Additional requirements–Speed signs
1. Engineering and traffic investigation   Done by private firm,
   No term. pts.
2. Township board of trustees resolution
3. Local authorities request
4. DOT acceptance
5. Terminal points
6. Major public roadway intersections

Traffic Signals	
1. Traffic study	Not done
2.Warrants	
3. Height	

Radar
1. Calibration   Internal and External Before
and after shift No log before
2. Officer training/competence
3. Proper set-up
4. Tracking history   Officer's visual
   Radar visual
   Radar audio

Producing Inconsistencies Checklist

1. Failed to include 4511.21(A) on traffic ticket. What to do? Argue driving reasonably under the circumstances. Motion to dismiss, cross-examination, motion for acquittal, closing argument.

2. [Failed to include 2151.021 on traffic ticket]. What to do? Wait until Prosecution rests, then motion for judgment of acquittal.

3. Traffic sign is only 5 ft 11 inches. What to do? Motion to dismiss ASAP.

4. Only witness to scene says saw male with brown hair. What to do? Insufficient identity. Cross examination, motion for acquittal, closing.

5. Officer's logbook incomplete. What to do? Cross-examination, motion for acquittal, closing

6. Engineering and traffic investigation done by private firm, and doesn't name terminal points. What to do? Motion to dismiss.

Notice Request

IN THE COURT OF COMMON PLEAS
[JUVENILE DIVISION]
X COUNTY, OHIO

IN THE MATTER OF:	:	CASE NO. CT 02-111
JOHN H. DOE:	:	JUDGE SCHMUCKATELLI
D/O/B: 8-27-67 [85]		
Alleged [Juvenile] Traffic Offender:	:	**REQUEST FOR NOTICE OF PROESECUTOR'S INTENT TO USE EVIDENCE**

Pursuant to Rule 11(D) of the Ohio Traffic Rules, I, John H. Doe, the Defendant, hereby request notice of the prosecuting attorney's intention to use evidence in chief at trial, which evidence I, the Defendant, am entitled to discover under Rule 16 of the Ohio Rules of Criminal Procedure [Rule 24 of the Ohio Rules of Juvenile Procedure].

John H. Doe
0000 Yuckalittle Drive
Ohio

Discovery Request

IN THE COURT OF COMMON PLEAS
[JUVENILE DIVISION]
X COUNTY, OHIO

IN THE MATTER OF:	:	CASE NO. CT 02-111
JOHN H. DOE:	:	JUDGE SCHMUCKATELLI
D/O/B: 8-27-67 [85]		
Alleged [Juvenile] Traffic Offender:	:	**REQUEST FOR DISCOVERY**

Pursuant to Rule 16(A)&(B) of the Ohio Rules of Criminal Procedure [Rule 24(A) of the Ohio Rules of Juvenile Procedure], I, John H. Doe, the Defendant, hereby request discovery of all information subject to disclosure under the above Rule.

_____
John H. Doe
0000 Yuckalittle Drive
Ohio

I hereby certify that a copy of the foregoing Request for Discovery was hand delivered to the prosecutor's office at (address of prosecutor's officer), this xxth day of February, 20xx.

_____
John H. Doe
0000 Yuckalittle Drive
Ohio

Discovery Request (E&T)

IN THE COURT OF COMMON PLEAS
[JUVENILE DIVISION]
X COUNTY, OHIO

IN THE MATTER OF: :   CASE NO. CT 02-111
JOHN H. DOE: :   JUDGE SCHMUCKATELLI
D/O/B: 8-27-67 [85]
Alleged [Juvenile] Traffic Offender: :   **REQUEST FOR
                                            DISCOVERY**

Pursuant to Rule 16(A)&(B) of the Ohio Rules of Criminal Procedure [Rule 24(A) of the Ohio Rules of Juvenile Procedure], I, John H. Doe, the Defendant, hereby request discovery of all information subject to disclosure under the above Rule.

This Discovery Request includes, but is not limited to, the following information:

(1) Any and all engineering and traffic investigations done for the area of roadway encompassing the speed zone, and/or containing the speed signs, used for establishing, or forming the basis of, the citation(s) in the above-captioned case.

(2) Any and all board of township trustee or other local authority resolutions declaring a speed limit or establishing a speed zone pursuant to the above-mentioned engineering and traffic investigation(s), or if not pursuant to any engineering and traffic investigation but nonetheless resolving to establish a speed zone or declare a speed limit in the above-mentioned area of roadway.

(3) Any and all board of township trustee or other local authority requests to the Ohio Department of Transportation and/or its agents requesting such speed limit or speed zone determinations be made by the Department and/or its agents.

(4)   Any and all Ohio Department of Transportation and/or its agent's declarations or determinations of aforesaid speed zone or acceptance or denial of aforesaid resolutions or requests or later withdrawals of such acceptance.

_____

John H. Doe
0000 Yuckalittle Drive
Ohio

I hereby certify that a copy of the foregoing Request for Discovery was hand delivered to the prosecutor's office at (address of prosecutor's officer), this xxth day of February, 20xx.

_____

John H. Doe
0000 Yuckalittle Drive
Ohio

Discovery Request (Speeding)

IN THE COURT OF COMMON PLEAS
[JUVENILE DIVISION]
X COUNTY, OHIO

IN THE MATTER OF:	:	CASE NO. CT 02-111
JOHN H. DOE:	:	JUDGE SCHMUCKATELLI
D/O/B: 8-27-67 [85]		
Alleged [Juvenile] Traffic Offender:	:	**REQUEST FOR**
		DISCOVERY

Pursuant to Rule 16(A)&(B) of the Ohio Rules of Criminal Procedure [Rule 24(A) of the Ohio Rules of Juvenile Procedure], I, John H. Doe, the Defendant, hereby request discovery of all information subject to disclosure under the above Rule. This Discovery Request includes, but is not limited to, the following information:

(1) Any and all logbooks used by the citing law enforcement officer in the above-captioned case or other officer(s) aiding in documenting such citation(s), including, but not limited to, the radar/laser/vascar calibration logbook, traffic logbook and shift logbook.

(2) Any and all law enforcement department, of which the aforesaid law enforcement officers are a part, policies or procedures pertaining to the type of radar/laser used in establishing the above-captioned citation(s), as to its calibration, operation, set-up or maintenance.

(3) Any and all operator, owner, maintenance, calibration or other manuals of the type of radar/laser used to establish the above-captioned citation(s), whether made by the aforesaid law enforcement department or by the radar/laser manufacturer.

(4)   Any and all maintenance or repair logs, or information concern-
      ing maintenance or repair, of the particular radar/laser used to
      establish the above-captioned citation(s).

_____
John H. Doe
0000 Yuckalittle Drive
Ohio

I hereby certify that a copy of the foregoing Request for Discovery was
hand delivered to the prosecutor's office at (address of prosecutor's officer), this xxth day of February, 20xx.

_____
John H. Doe
0000 Yuckalittle Drive
Ohio

Motion for Discovery

IN THE COURT OF COMMON PLEAS
[JUVENILE DIVISION]
X COUNTY, OHIO

IN THE MATTER OF:	:	CASE NO. CT 02-111
JOHN H. DOE:	:	JUDGE SCHMUCKATELLI
D/O/B: 8-27-67 [85]		
Alleged [Juvenile] Traffic Offender:	:	**MOTION FOR DISCOVERY**

Pursuant to Rule 16(A)&(B) of the Ohio Rules of Criminal Procedure [Rule 24(A)&(B) of the Ohio Rules of Juvenile Procedure], I, John H. Doe, the Defendant, hereby Motion for Discovery of all information subject to disclosure under the above Rule. This Motion for Discovery includes, but is not limited to, the following information:

(1)   Any and all logbooks used by the citing law enforcement officer in the above-captioned case or other officer(s) aiding in documenting such citation(s), including, but not limited to, the radar/laser/vascar calibration logbook, traffic logbook and shift logbook.

(2)   Any and all law enforcement department, of which the aforesaid law enforcement officers are a part, policies or procedures pertaining to the type of radar/laser used in establishing the above-captioned citation(s), as to its calibration, operation, set-up or maintenance.

(3)   Any and all operator, owner, maintenance, calibration or other manuals of the type of radar/laser used to establish the above-captioned citation(s), whether made by the aforesaid law enforcement department or by the radar/laser manufacturer.

(4) Any and all maintenance or repair logs, or information concerning maintenance or repair, of the particular radar/laser used to establish the above-captioned citation(s).

(5) Any and all engineering and traffic investigations done for the area of roadway encompassing the speed zone, and/or containing the speed signs, used for establishing, or forming the basis of, the citation(s) in the above-captioned case.

(6) Any and all board of township trustee or other local authority resolutions declaring a speed limit or establishing a speed zone pursuant to the above-mentioned engineering and traffic investigation(s), or if not pursuant to any engineering and traffic investigation but nonetheless resolving to establish a speed zone or declare a speed limit in the above-mentioned area of roadway.

(7) Any and all board of township trustee or other local authority requests to the Ohio Department of Transportation and/or its agents requesting such speed limit or speed zone determinations be made by the Department and/or its agents.

(8) Any and all Ohio Department of Transportation and/or its agent's declarations or determinations of aforesaid speed zone or acceptance or denial of aforesaid resolutions or requests or later withdrawals of such acceptance.

John H. Doe
0000 Yuckalittle Drive
Ohio

I hereby certify that demand for discovery has been made via a Discovery Request pursuant to Rule 16(A)&(B) of the Ohio Rules of Criminal Procedure [Rule 24(A) of the Ohio Rules of Juvenile

Procedure], but that such request was denied or ignored and the discovery has not been provided.

_____

John H. Doe
0000 Yuckalittle Drive
Ohio

I hereby certify that a copy of the foregoing Motion for Discovery was hand delivered to the prosecutor's office at (address of prosecutor's officer), this xxth day of February, 20xx.

_____

John H. Doe
0000 Yuckalittle Drive
Ohio

Motion for Production

IN THE COURT OF COMMON PLEAS
[JUVENILE DIVISION]
X COUNTY, OHIO

IN THE MATTER OF:	:	CASE NO. CT 02-111
JOHN H. DOE:	:	JUDGE SCHMUCKATELLI
D/O/B: 8-27-67 [85]		
Alleged [Juvenile] Traffic Offender:	:	MOTION FOR
		PRODUCTION

Now comes the Defendant, John H. Doe, in the above-captioned case, to preserve my rights in trial and for appeal, and so hereby moves the Court to issue an order requiring the government to produce the following information and documents at the trial for the above captioned case:

(1) and all logbooks used by the citing law enforcement officer in the above-captioned case or other officer(s) aiding in documenting such citation(s), including, but not limited to, the radar/laser/vascar calibration logbook, traffic logbook and shift logbook.

(2) Any and all law enforcement department, of which the aforesaid law enforcement officers are a part, policies or procedures pertaining to the type of radar/laser used in establishing the above-captioned citation(s), as to its calibration, operation, set-up or maintenance.

(3) Any and all operator, owner, maintenance, calibration or other manuals of the type of radar/laser used to establish the above-captioned citation(s), whether made by the aforesaid law enforcement department or by the radar/laser manufacturer.

(4) Any and all maintenance or repair logs, or information concerning maintenance or repair, of the particular radar/laser used to establish the above-captioned citation(s).

(5) Any and all engineering and traffic investigations done for the area of roadway encompassing the speed zone, and/or containing the speed signs, used for establishing, or forming the basis of, the citation(s) in the above-captioned case.

(6) Any and all board of township trustee or other local authority resolutions declaring a speed limit or establishing a speed zone pursuant to the above-mentioned engineering and traffic investigation(s), or if not pursuant to any engineering and traffic investigation but nonetheless resolving to establish a speed zone or declare a speed limit in the above-mentioned area of roadway.

(7) Any and all board of township trustee or other local authority requests to the Ohio Department of Transportation and/or its agents requesting such speed limit or speed zone determinations be made by the Department and/or its agents.

(8) Any and all Ohio Department of Transportation and/or its agent's declarations or determinations of aforesaid speed zone or acceptance or denial of aforesaid resolutions or requests or later withdrawals of such acceptance.

(9) Any and all traffic studies done for installation of the traffic signal used in establishing the citation of the above captioned case.

(10) Official Department of Public Safety documentation of the bus driver's bus driving license and documentation of the buses registration and inspection verification with the superintendent of the state highway patrol.

John H. Doe
0000 Yuckalittle Drive
Ohio

Motion to Dismiss (Defect in ticket, E&T, Signs)

IN THE COURT OF COMMON PLEAS
[JUVENILE DIVISION]
X COUNTY, OHIO

IN THE MATTER OF:	:	CASE NO. CT 02-111
JOHN H. DOE:	:	JUDGE SCHMUCKATELLI
D/O/B: 8-27-67 [85]		
Alleged [Juvenile] Traffic Offender:	:	**MOTION TO**
		DISMISS

Now comes the Defendant, John H. Doe, in the above-captioned case, and moves to dismiss the above-captioned case, and ticket and charge for the above-captioned case, with prejudice on the following grounds and arguments:

(1) *There is a defect in the ticket.* The ticket does not correctly cite to the statutory provision that is claimed violated. The ticket cites §4511.43(A), which concerns the right-of-way at stop signs. The officer's remarks, and the enclosed photograph of the subject intersection, show a yield sign located at the intersection, which requires citation under §4511.43(B), vice §4511.43(A). Since the ticket cannot be amended to correct for such error without changing the name and identity of the crime charged, which Rule 7(D) of the Ohio Rules of Criminal Procedure prohibit, there can be no amendment and the above-captioned case must be dismissed with prejudice.

(2) *No engineering and traffic investigation was done.* Speed limit signs mark the speed zone of the roadway I was ticketed on as thirty-five miles per hour. This speed zone can only be legally established and enforced pursuant to an engineering and traffic investigation and subsequent official resolutions and/or Department of Transportation acceptance of speed zone

requests. *See* 4511.21(J)(K)(I). Though discovery was requested and motioned for concerning such documents, and though the Defendant has personally attempted to acquire such documents, no documents exist or can be found showing that an engineering and traffic investigation or any board of trustee resolution or local authority request was in fact done. As such, the above-captioned case should be dismissed with prejudice.

(3) *The applicable traffic sign does not meet OMUTCD requirements.* The Ohio Manual of Uniform Traffic and Control Devices requires, among other things, that signs in residential areas were pedestrian traffic is likely to occur must measure at least seven feet measured from the bottom of the sign to the plane level with the top of the curb. *See* OMUTCD, §2E–4(Rev. 20). As the enclosed photograph and affidavit of the person standing next to the sign in the photograph show, the sign is only five feet eleven inches in height. It is therefore an unofficial traffic sign and as such is unenforceable. *See* §§4511.11(D), 4511.12¶2. As this traffic control device forms the basis for establishment of the citation against me, the above-captioned case should be dismissed with prejudice.

_____

John H. Doe
0000 Yuckalittle Drive
Ohio

I hereby certify that a copy of the foregoing Motion to Dismiss was hand delivered to the prosecutor's office at (address of prosecutor's officer), this xxth day of February, 20xx.

_____

John H. Doe
0000 Yuckalittle Drive
Ohio

Request for Continuance

IN THE COURT OF COMMON PLEAS
[JUVENILE DIVISION]
X COUNTY, OHIO

IN THE MATTER OF:	:	CASE NO. CT 02-111
JOHN H. DOE:	:	JUDGE SCHMUCKATELLI
D/O/B: 8-27-67 [85]		
Alleged [Juvenile] Traffic Offender:	:	**REQUEST FOR**
		CONTINUANCE

Pursuant to Rule 18 of the Ohio Rules of Criminal Procedure [Rule 23 of the Ohio Rules of Juvenile Procedure], I, John H. Doe, the Defendant, hereby request a continuance for the above-captioned case on the following grounds. [My parents will be out of town during the time period the trial date is set, namely March 5th.] I will be out of town on a business trip for the week containing the trial date. Enclosed is a letter from my supervisor attesting to this fact. For this reason, I respectfully request a continuance of the trial for the above-captioned case to a time period after…

_____

John H. Doe
0000 Yuckalittle Drive
Ohio

Notes

Preface

1 *The Canton Repository, Wrong signs for speed limits posted in Plain* (Sep 28, 2001), and *Township has its own illegal agenda on speed limits* (Oct 18, 2001).

2 *The Canton Repository, State believes New Rome speed limit is illegal* (Jun 13, 2002).

3 *Dayton Daily News, Former New Rome clerk sentenced* (Jun 16, 2002).

4 *CNN/Money, The need for $peed—it will cost you!* (May 24, 2002).

5 *The Canton Repository, State believes New Rome speed limit is illegal* (Jun 13, 2002).

6 Alan Dershowitz, *Letters to a Young Lawyer* (2001) p. 80.

7 *Id.* p. 79-80.

Chapter 10: All tickets based on traffic signs

8 *The Canton Repository, Speed limits lowered on three Jackson roads* (Sep 11, 2001).

9 *The Canton Repository, Lower speed limit recommended in Plain Twp.* (Oct 10, 2001).

10 *CNN/Money, The need for $peed—it will cost you!* (May 24, 2002).

0-595-21521-1

Made in the USA
Lexington, KY
02 November 2017